I fell in love over New Yor[k]
breakfasts over
I dropped
my faith   in god and
became   what you
wanted.   I freed my
nd wept.   I never felt
so lost and alone. And
ow I've returned
nger wiser
and have never fallen in love
So deep again since
Somewhere inside I'm still
eeling, or maybe I've hardened

KRAFT
GRAPE
JELLY
INGREDIENTS: SUGAR, WATER
GRAPE JUICE CONCENTRATE
FRUIT PECTIN, CITRIC ACID

UNITED STATES
OF AMERICA · VISA
ISSUING POST/AUTH
LONDON
Surname
LIGHTMAN
Given name
SARAH

THE
BOOK
OF
SARAH

Susan Merrill Squier and Ian Williams, *General Editors*

Editorial Collective
MK Czerwiec (Northwestern University)
Michael J. Green (Penn State University College of Medicine)
Kimberly R. Myers (Penn State University College of Medicine)
Scott T. Smith (Penn State University)

Books in the Graphic Medicine series are inspired by a growing awareness of the value of comics as an important resource for communicating about a range of issues broadly termed "medical." For healthcare practitioners, patients, families, and caregivers dealing with illness and disability, graphic narrative enlightens complicated or difficult experience. For scholars in literary, cultural, and comics studies, the genre articulates a complex and powerful analysis of illness, medicine, and disability and a rethinking of the boundaries of "health." The series includes original comics from artists and non-artists alike, such as self-reflective "graphic pathographies" or comics used in medical training and education, as well as monographic studies and edited collections from scholars, practitioners, and medical educators.

Other titles in the series:

MK Czerwiec, Ian Williams, Susan Merrill Squier, Michael J. Green, Kimberly R. Myers, and Scott T. Smith, *Graphic Medicine Manifesto*

Ian Williams, *The Bad Doctor: The Troubled Life and Times of Dr. Iwan James*

Peter Dunlap-Shohl, *My Degeneration: A Journey Through Parkinson's*

Aneurin Wright, *Things to Do in a Retirement Home Trailer Park: . . . When You're 29 and Unemployed*

Dana Walrath, *Aliceheimers: Alzheimer's Through the Looking Glass*

Lorenzo Servitje and Sherryl Vint, eds., *The Walking Med: Zombies and the Medical Image*

Henny Beaumont, *Hole in the Heart: Bringing Up Beth*

MK Czerwiec, *Taking Turns: Stories From Unit 371*

Paula Knight, *The Facts of Life*

Gareth Brookes, *A Thousand Coloured Castles*

Jenell Johnson, ed., *Graphic Reproduction: A Comics Anthology*

Olivier Kugler, *Escaping Wars and Waves: Encounters with Syrian Refugees*

Judith Margolis, *Life Support: Invitation to Prayer*

Ian Williams, *The Lady Doctor*

THE
BOOK
OF
SARAH

Sarah Lightman

The Pennsylvania State University Press

University Park, Pennsylvania

Cataloging-in-publication data is on file with
the Library of Congress.

Copyright © 2019 Sarah Lightman
All rights reserved
Printed in Poland
www.lfbookservices.co.uk
Published by The Pennsylvania State University Press,
University Park, PA 16802-1003
First published by Myriad Editions,
www.myriadeditions.com

The Pennsylvania State University Press is a member
of the Association of University Presses.

It is the policy of The Pennsylvania State University
Press to use acid-free paper. Publications on uncoated
stock satisfy the minimum requirements of American
National Standard for Information Sciences –
Permanence of Paper for Printed Library Material,
ANSI Z39.48-1992.

Cover and book interior designed by
Woodrow Phoenix

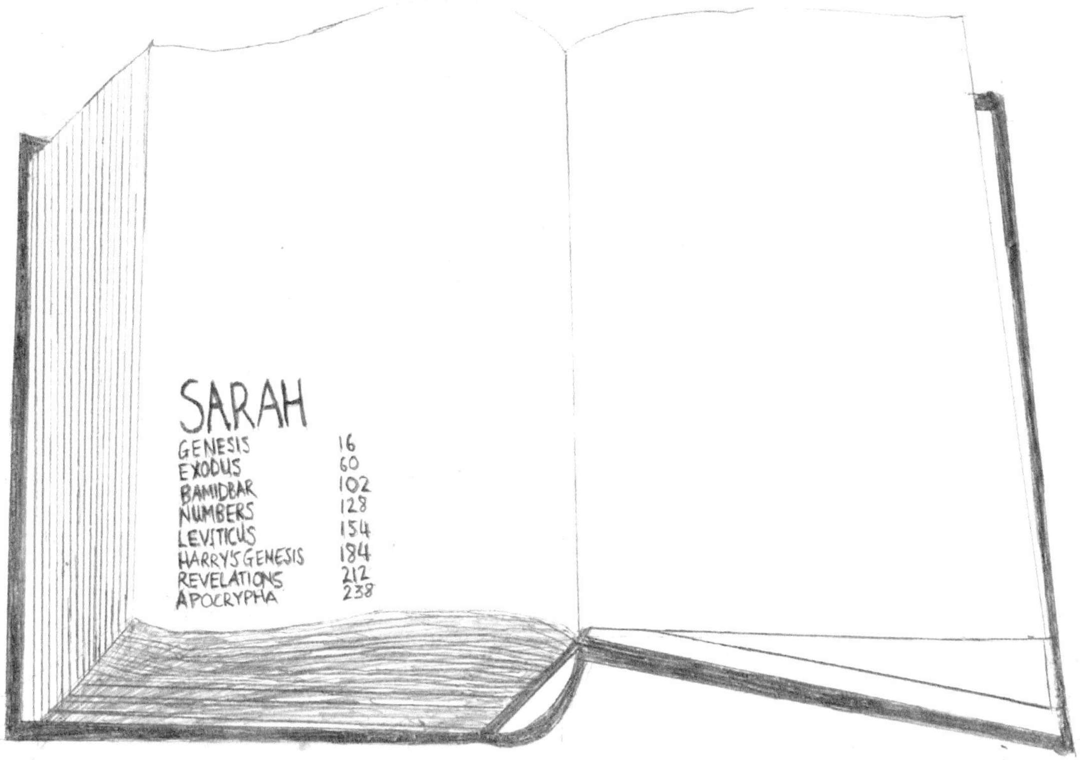
SARAH
GENESIS 16
EXODUS 60
BAMIDBAR 102
NUMBERS 128
LEVITICUS 154
HARRY'S GENESIS 184
REVELATIONS 212
APOCRYPHA 238

It is a cold, blue-sky winter's day in my studio in Holborn.
I am finishing off a new series of paintings, tracing in colour
my experiences of motherhood.

I'd rather spend money on my art than trying to get pregnant again

It feels wonderful to paint, to make art, to have friends in the studio building.

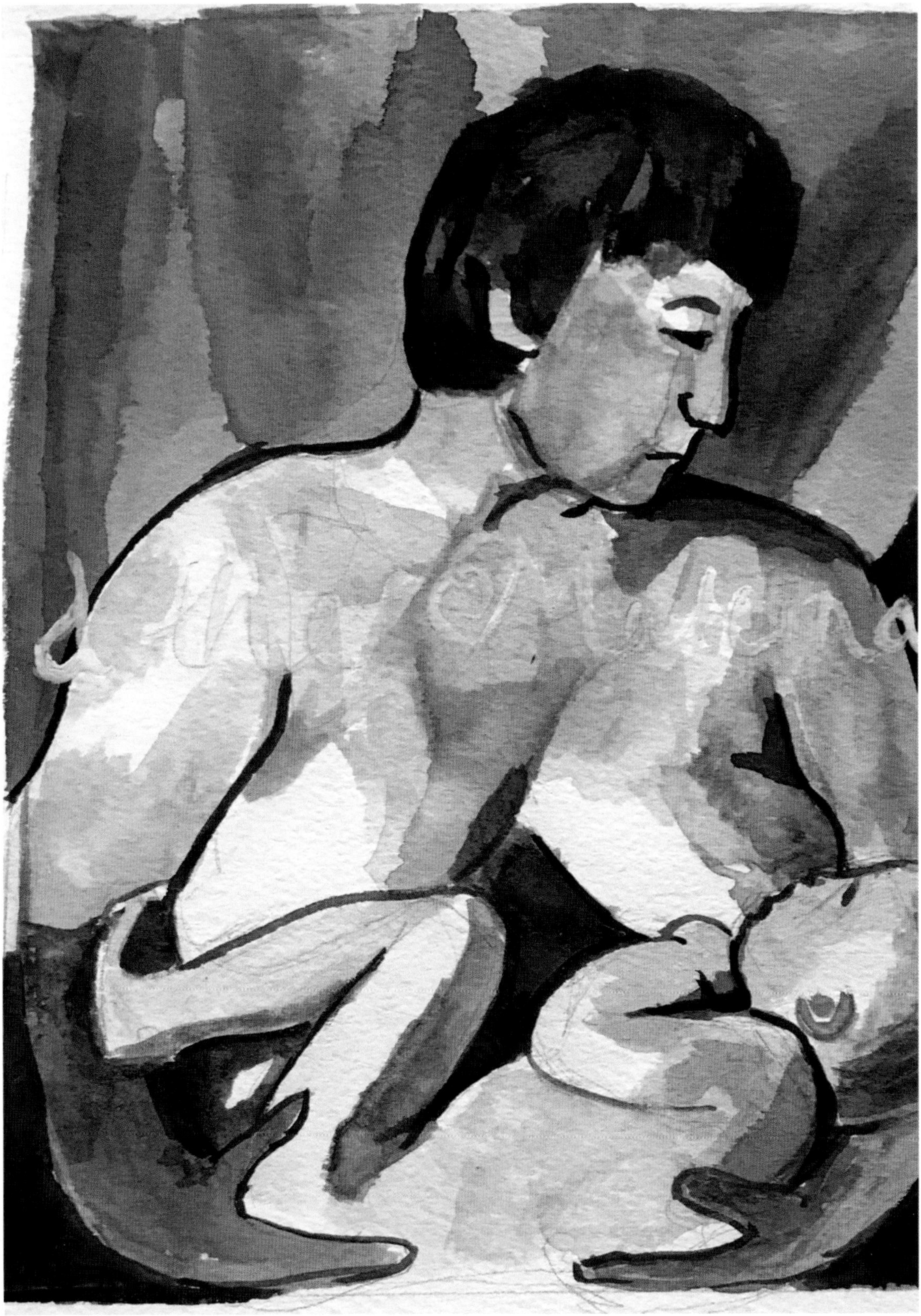

Since you can now swim

I'll Keep this for my own buoyancy

You outgrow

I outgrow friends

shoes.

s religious beliefs

Every morning, during my first three years at the Slade School
of Art, I would read from that week's portion of the Torah, a
passage from the Books of Moses that is read out in synagogues
and changes each week. I would mark down my questions and
comments in the margins.

כג (א) וַיִּהְיוּ חַיֵּי שָׂרָה מֵאָה שָׁנָה וְעֶשְׂרִים
שָׁנָה וְשֶׁבַע שָׁנִים שְׁנֵי חַיֵּי שָׂרָה:

רש"י כג (א) ויהיו חיי שרה כלחיד

רש"י כג (א) ויהיו חיי שרה.
רצ"פ מבטאר בשרה לא נתפרש
אצל חיין יהוצד הוצרך לפרש
ימי חייך יהוצד לקזכיר מיתתה
בשבריך הבייך המצדה, בדרש בתד
בתה לאחד תשעים של הודתה,

רמב"ן כג (א) מאה שנה ועשרים
שנה, ושבע דש"יך לכך נכתב
שנה בכל כלל לומר לך שכל אחד
נדרש לצעמו, בת מאה כבת
עשרים לחטא, ובת עשרים כבת
שבע ליופי.

כג (א) ויהיו חיי שרה
מאה שנה ועשרים שרה
רעשרים שנה וצטרים שנה
לכך בכתב בה רשבע שנה
וקלל לומר לך שכל בכל כלל
לצצמו בת בת של אחד כלל
מה בת ובת הקבת ני כחברן
בת צדנש לא הקבת ני לחטא
חטא, ובת כי, כבת כי הדראת
שני חדת כי, ובת קיבלא
לטובה שרה, כלן שרה.

And then I would travel on the tube to the Slade
and show my drawings of my own life story.

The Book of Sarah
(1:1)
The Life of Sarah

The Life of Sarah: And these were the days of the life of Sarah when she reached her 23rd year.

The Life of Sarah: The life of Sarah - that is the Book of Sarah.

The Life of Sarah: And they said to her: There is no Book of Sarah. But is there not a Book of Esther and a Book of Daniel? she asked. And they said: But you have a whole section of the Torah named after you, and the Torah is holier than the Writings of the Prophets. But still she demanded a Book of Sarah.

GENESIS
IN MY BEGINNING

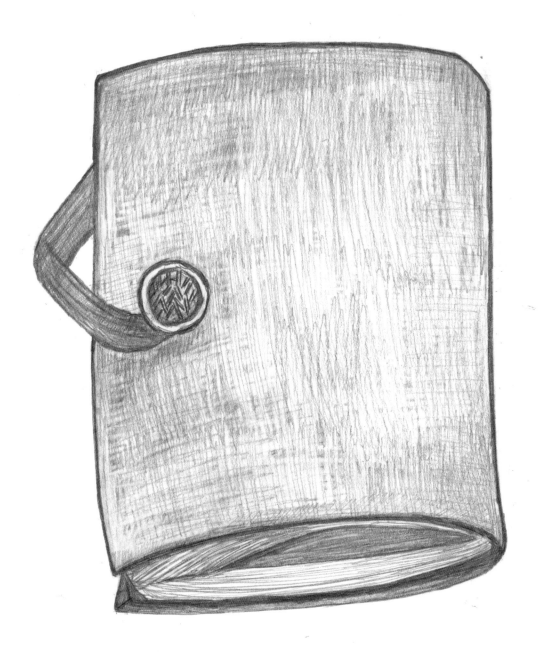

I was given a diary for my tenth birthday and I would write in it every night. My self-scribed beginning. For years afterwards, I kept more and more of these diaries, bubbling with thoughts, desires and dark secrets. Back then, my diaries were the only place I had to speak of feelings, because, as a family, we never really spoke of them at all.

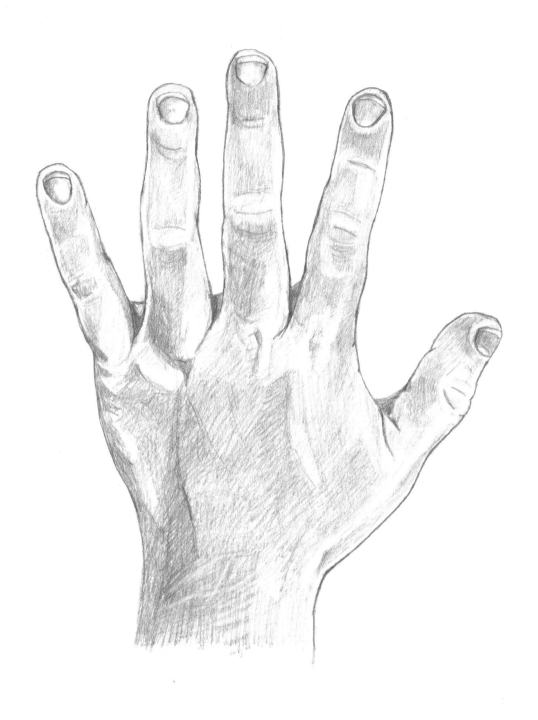

In my early years, at night, after I said the Shema, the bedtime prayers, I would ask God to bless my whole family. I'd look up through the skylight and count them all off on my fingers.

My Mum and Dad.

My sister Esther and brother Daniel.

My maternal Granny and Grandpa who lived down the road.

My paternal Grandma and Pop, in Lincoln's Inn, and their housekeeper, Mrs Leahy.

It was quite a long list, but I felt my prayers were keeping
everyone safe. In my home there was a constant fear of people
dying, so perhaps my prayers really worked. By my mid-twenties,
when I had long stopped praying, my grandparents started dying.
Now, only one grandmother survives.

My father's father's family wasn't supposed to have ended up in England. Their story, like that of many other Jewish immigrants, is that they got off the boat from Vilna too soon. They were told at Liverpool that this was New York, where they had paid to travel. I saw in Ellis Island records that other members of the family did actually make it there.

I'm writing this to understand how much my heart wanted me to stay in New York, that time fifteen years ago. And how, maybe, it is just in my genes not to make it.

Still, I am grateful for any family that made the journey at all. Lichtmakhers were amongst those killed in the Vilna Ghetto. And my great-grandfather in Leeds mentioned two sisters in his will; two he left back in Vilna, whom he never heard from again.

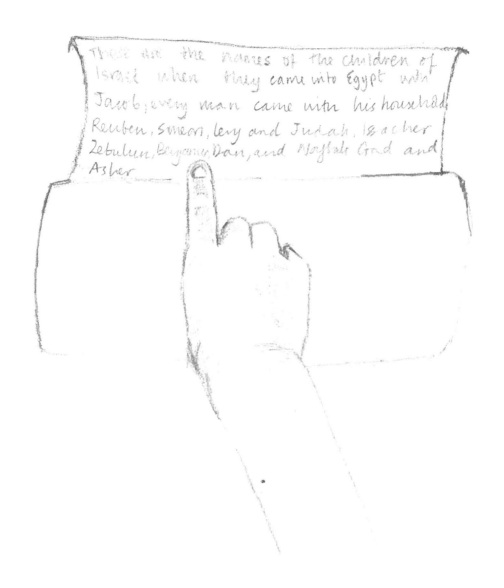

These are the names of the children of Israel when they came into Egypt with Jacob; every man came with his household. Reuben, Simeon, Levy and Judah. Issacher Zebulun, Benjamin Dan, and Naftali Gad and Asher

On my mother's side, Harold Claff, a GP who was a ship's doctor in the Navy during the Second World War, never made the written work he longed to create; his last name, Claff, like the parchment used for the sefer torah.

At art school I created a Scroll of Sarah; my own sefer torah that began with how I had shared a name with two great-grandmothers.

I asked myself, how could I draw a book of my life, when I didn't know who I was? If I couldn't hear my own voice over all the others that surrounded me? It was a strong start to a book I didn't know how to end.

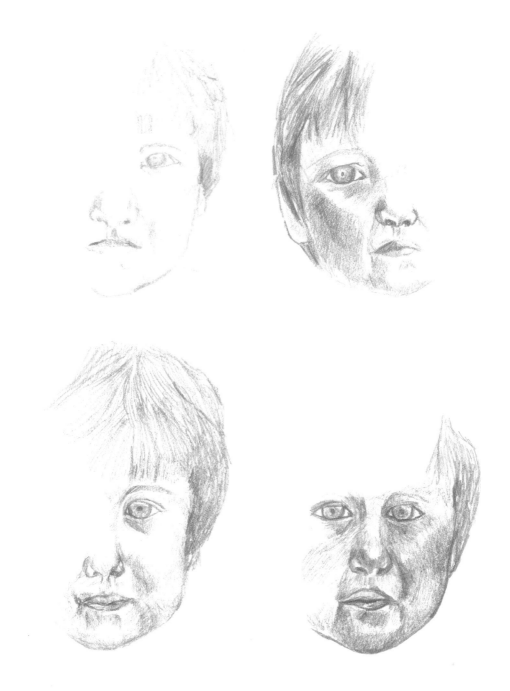

This is not my whole family's story. Just an attempt at my own.
But of course, their story is woven indelibly into my own, like
folktales, and bible stories, magical, impossible, and true. If I have
inherited short-sightedness and a propensity to allergies, then
why should I not also have inherited a self-thwarting mechanism,
an unfulfilled intellectualism, and both over-controlling and
over-dependent tendencies?

11 New End; the home the family lived in before I was born.

Dynamics and tensions are ossified in stories repeated through the years, traditional retellings at family meals and in front of new friends.

The frequently reiterated incident of Daniel trying to poke out Esther's eyes with a wooden horse when she was born.

There was the summer of love '74, when my parents had a
wonderful holiday in Switzerland. Every day, my mum played
with Esther on the hotel lawn, and my father took Daniel down
to swim by the lake.
I was born nine months later.

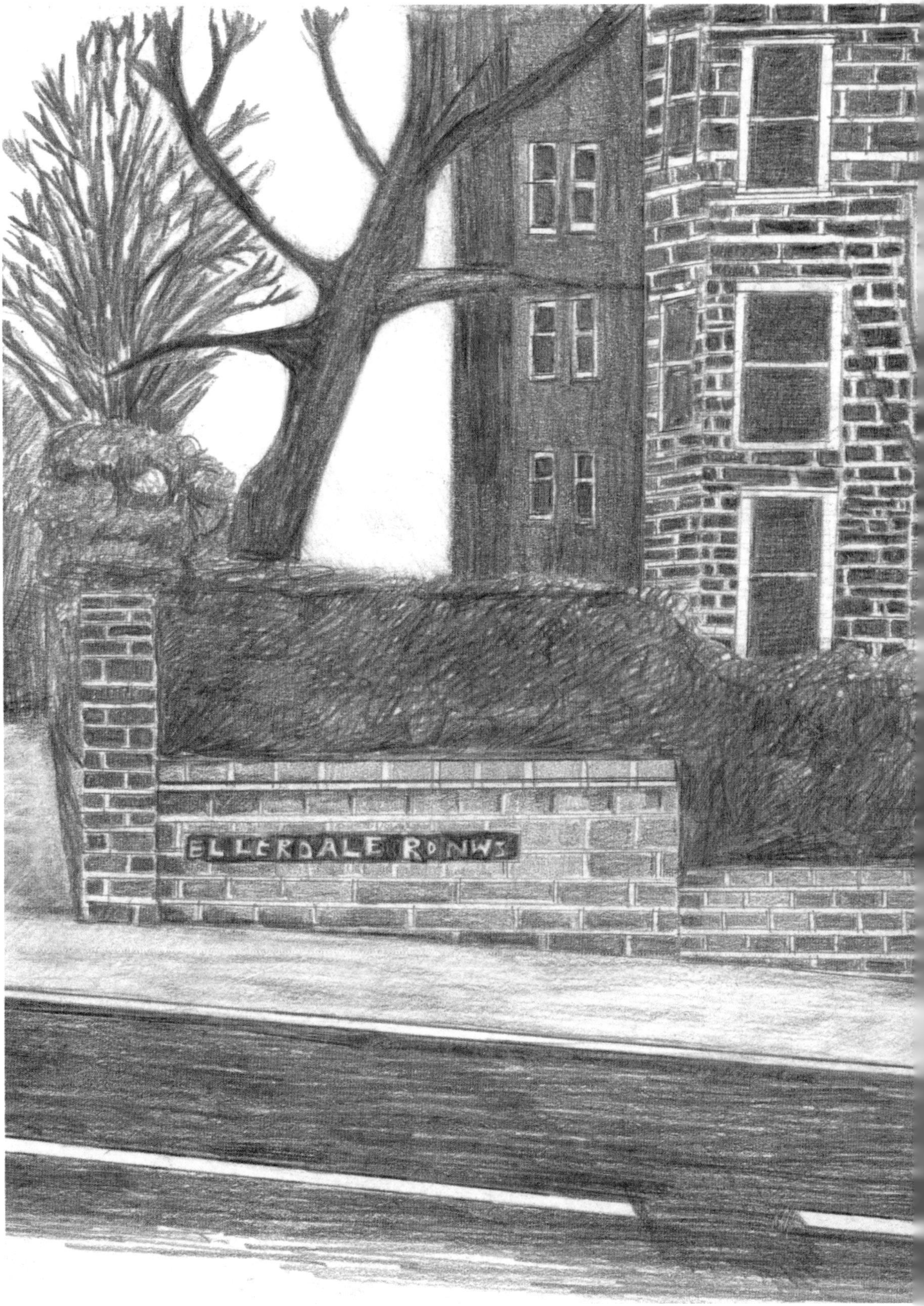
ELLERDALE RD NW3

Ellerdale Road: 1975 and 2013.

My son Harry and I share this address on our birth certificates.

Ethics of the Mothers:
my mother, Naomi, daughter of Daphne, used to say:
'Life is just swings and roundabouts.'

Harry, at least, would know about swings. (His favourite outing.) The thrill, the sense of flight. The inevitable decline. The journey that always leads back home.

I shared a room with Esther, crawling into her bed at night. I was already looking for something from someone else, coupled with an uncertain anxiety about inhabiting my own space.

And now, every night, we hear the door creak, then shuffling footsteps, as Harry climbs into our bed. He demands we hold his hand as he makes himself comfortable in between our two pillows. Then my husband, Charlie, exhausted, creeps into the spare room for some uninterrupted sleep.

At art school, showing artwork about home to the outside world was a way to keep one foot back in Hampstead.

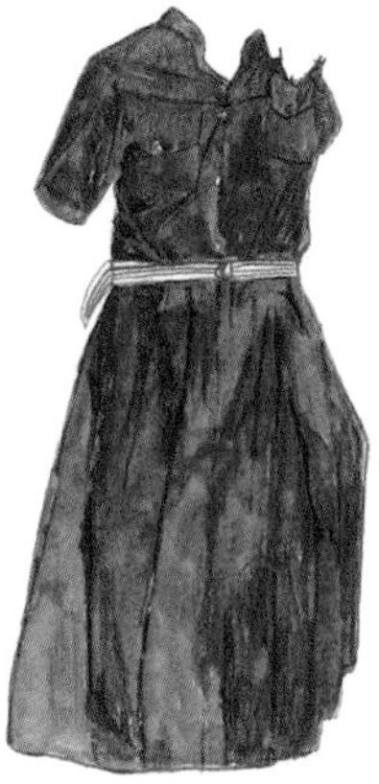

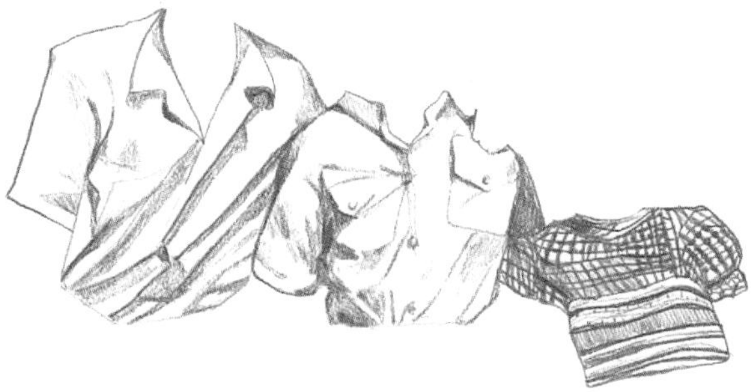

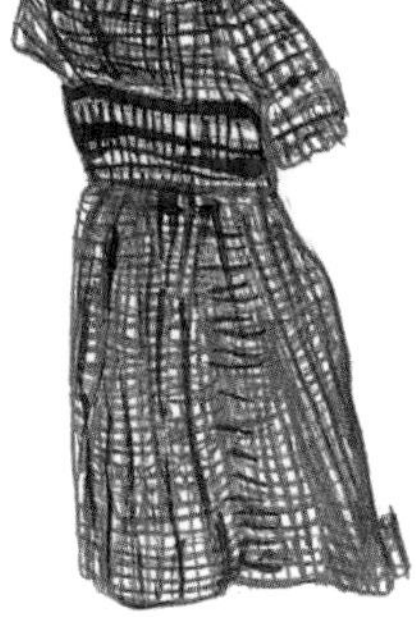

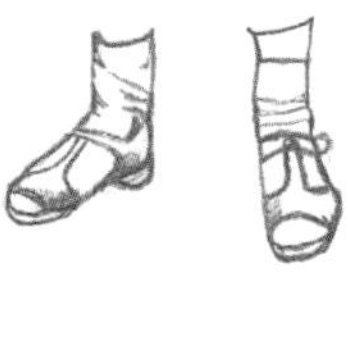

Families are like glass.

You see yourself and reality through them.

Constructing yourself...

in an already established community.

Mummy said Daniel will
never find a girl to marry...

who is as good
as his sisters.

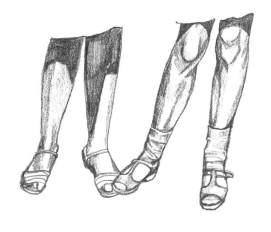

I don't think Daniel ever got over
the shock of me learning Latin.

Wearing Esther's shoes didn't
help me understand myself.

Moving out of home was supposed to define where I was propped up and to help me stand up on my own.

Perhaps all I did was recreate the world I left behind. Put us all together in the same room and nothing's changed.

I suppose I still needed propping up.

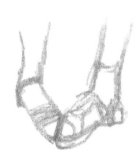

And I still squashed Esther a bit.

It was strange to be drawing my family from photos, when they were all living around me. But I couldn't draw them face on.

Like a bright light, only looking away reveals it.

Years later, my tutor said of my obvious unhappiness: 'We should have helped you more.' When she told me this, I hardly understood what she meant. At the time I'd felt supported, noted, recognized, and I hadn't known what I was missing. I'd been unhappy for so long that I thought it was part of my identity.

Last weekend, I asked my friend Maureen how I should deal with this feeling of shame and sadness about those incomplete years. She says I should be more understanding of my younger self.

'Once,' she explained to me, 'I met my younger self and I told her she was going to be an artist and that helped her.'

Look Sarah, look what you will become. It will get better. Not perfect, but better.

5b Prince Arthur Road; my childhood home.

It still inhabits my dreams.

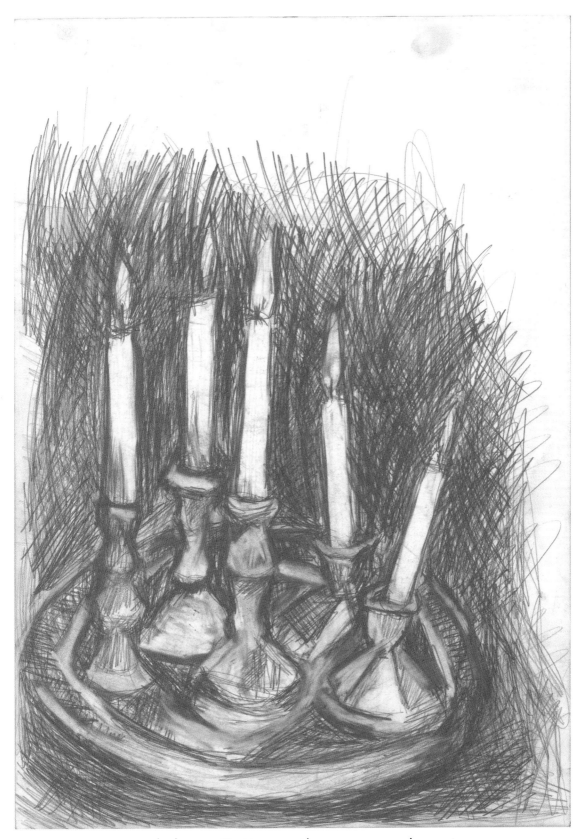

Inside, we would light a Shabbat candle for every family member.

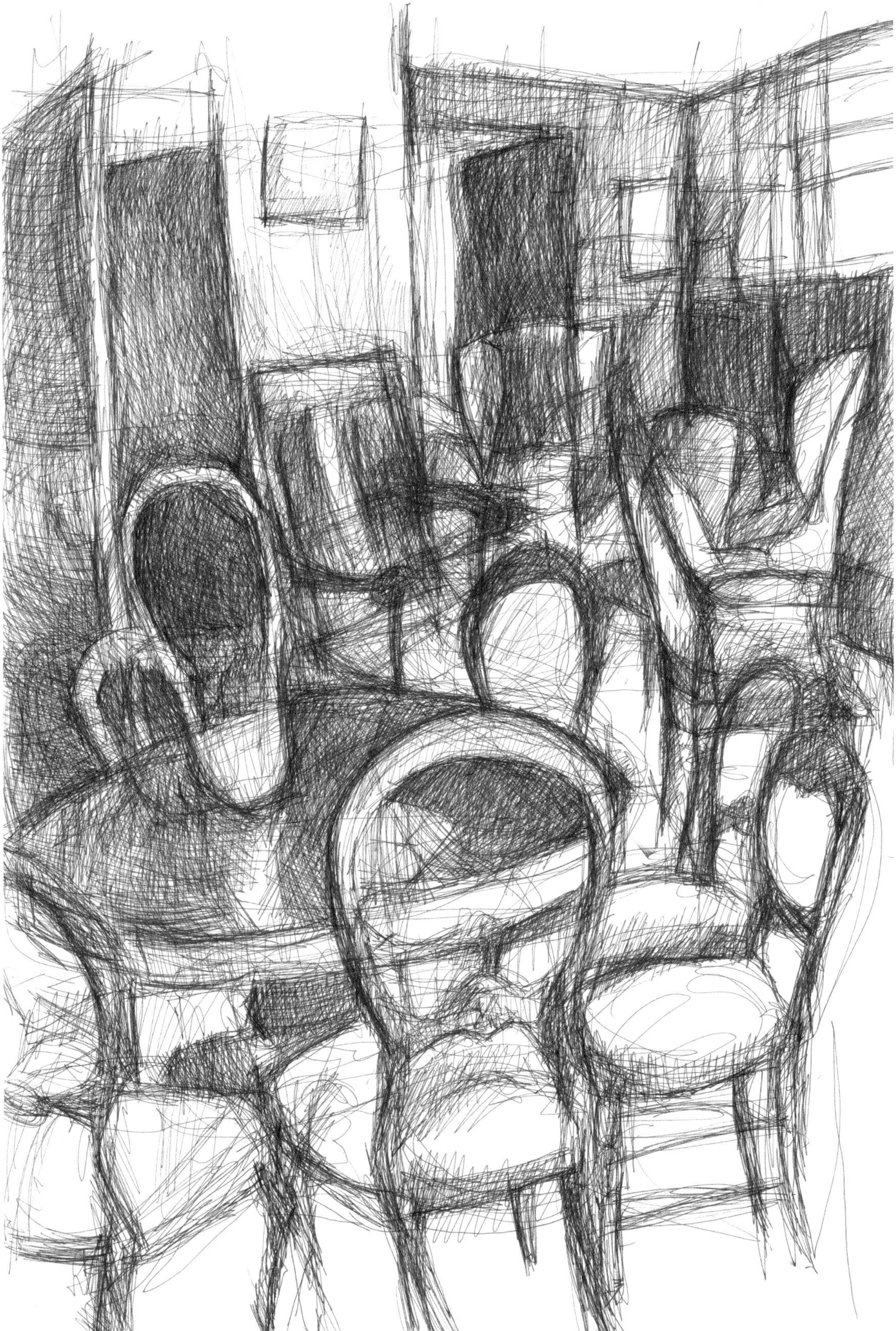

How good and pleasant it is when brothers and sisters sit together.

How good and pleasant it is when brothers and sisters
and mothers and fathers sit together.

How good and pleasant it is when brothers and sisters and
mothers and fathers and grannies and grandpas sit together.

(Though sometimes not so pleasant.)

For three weeks after my sister's wedding, we had a full house.
Then my grandfather died.

At the end of his shiva, the week of mourning, I laid the
Friday night table on a Wednesday. A midweek memorial
to a Friday night that would never happen again.

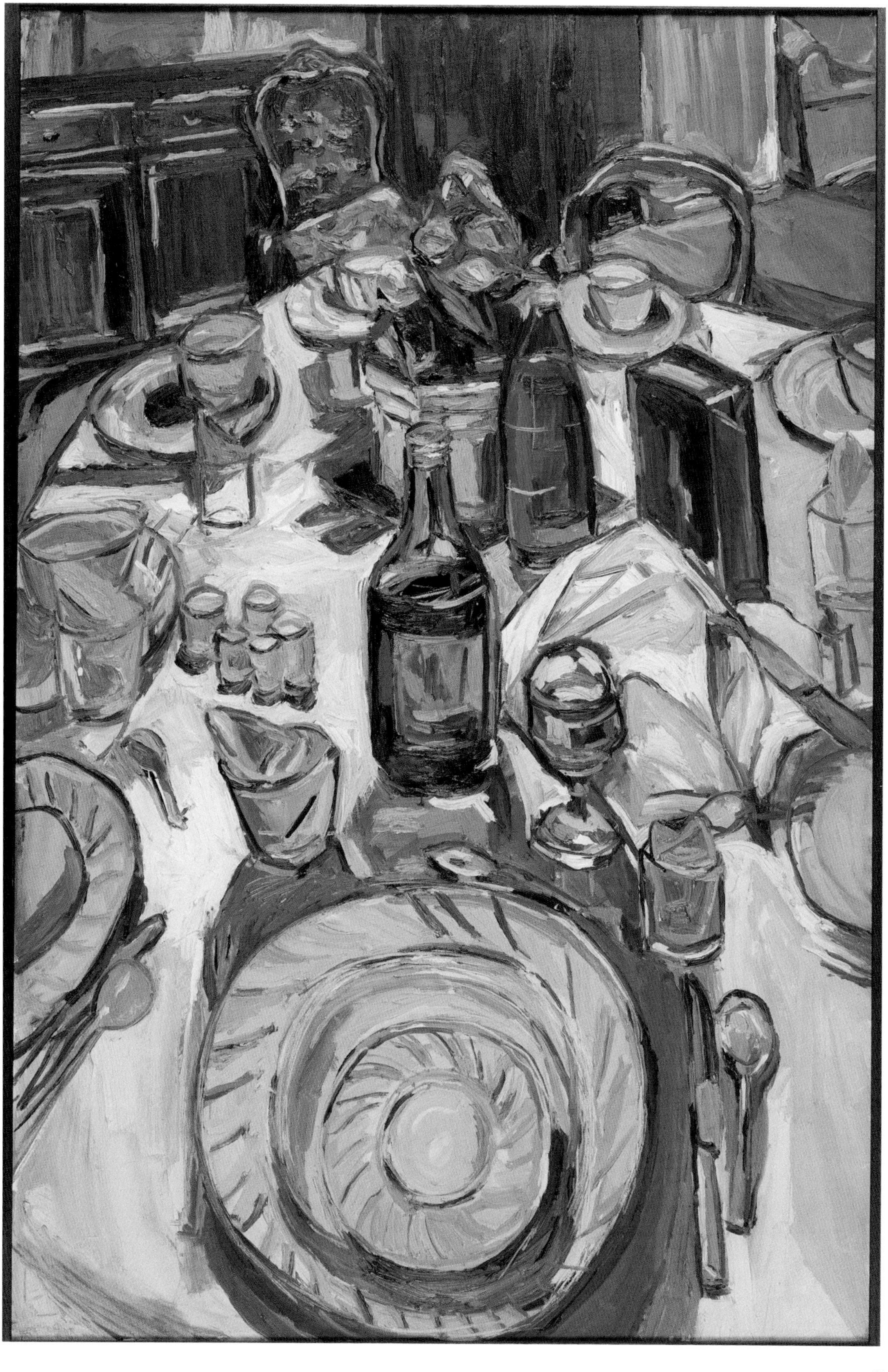

I wasn't considered up to much at St Paul's School for
Girls. I watched in wonder as people became themselves,
whilst I clung to others to find my own way.

At assemblies, the great ones were awarded, appointed and celebrated. I would watch and grow smaller in my own eyes, and theirs.

One parents' evening, there was a knock on
the locked door of my consciousness.

'Is Sarah happy at home?' asked my biology teacher. 'Of course she is,' retorted my mother as she dragged a silent me away.

My weekdays were spent at St Paul's, but my teenage self came alive with my Jewish friends on weekends.

Travelling back and forth between Hampstead and Golders Green, I was welcomed into their homes. This was happiness.

Every Shabbat we were together, eating food cooked by someone else's mother, talking about boys, clothes, laughing at each other.

One stop on the Northern Line, a lifetime of Jewish experience away.

I would force my father to put on a kippah, the Jewish
skullcap, as soon as he stepped off the tube at Golders Green.

I was desperate to be judged kindly by these more Orthodox Jews.
I was aching to belong, to be like them. Which I clearly was not.

On a recent Sunday night, we drove by on our way to dinner at a kosher restaurant. I caught a shadow of a passing memory; a casually-broken heart in the wastelands of Golders Green bus garage. Incidental monuments to my painful histories, pitted like acne scars.

Of course, none of my friends live here now.
They have all moved on.

All except me.

EXODUS
GO FORTH: AND BACK

Go forth, to the land I will show you. Leave your birthplace,
your family, your parents' house.

Oh Hendon. The house I didn't live in, with the boyfriend I didn't marry.

When university came along, my Jewish friends moved away, replacing me with fiancés, student digs and May balls. I tried to recreate what I had lost, but without the people. I covered my loneliness with a veneer of Orthodoxy and entered a religious cul-de-sac. I prayed much, I covered my body in shapeless skirts. Avoided love, and hardly broke into the chaotic disco dances for which I had been famed.

I lived at home and just drew my parents.

I hid out in my studio in my parents' garden, and, there, with
Charlotte Salomon as company, I began to find my voice. Finally,
it was I who won prizes. But I still couldn't make art amongst
other students, and I only made one friend. I dreamt of American
universities, of letting go of who I'd become, of starting a new life.

In 1999, in between my two degrees, I stayed with a friend in Brooklyn. I'd invited him to Seder at my parents' house years before. He said our parents had the same books on their shelves. He'd been writing letters to me, but I'd hardly noticed his interest in my fragile cocoon.

From disinterest to a love so strong I was overwhelmed. Zero to sixty. The first time he kissed me I just froze. I hadn't realised he liked me like that. I ate nothing but an apple for the next few days.

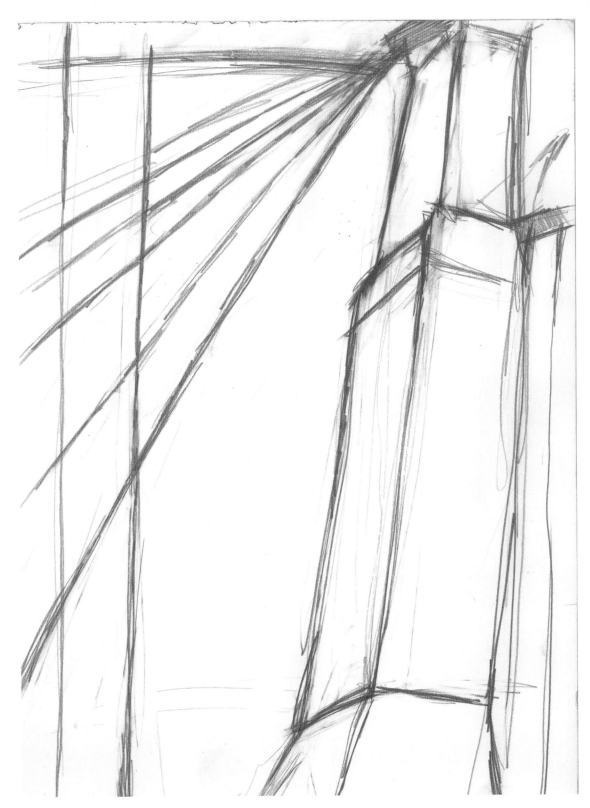

With Brooklyn Bridge, it was love at first sight. This was the New World. It was where people met or came together, or paths just crossed, against the constant thump of traffic.

I worried endlessly that love might not last. I wrote in my diary
'A love affair in the streets of New York comes to nothing (goes
nowhere?). A love affair in the streets of New York is holding on to
emptiness of street numbers, looking just for one place to settle.'

I loved being Jewish in New York. I felt alive. And unanchored.

Bernini
The Rape of
Proserpina.

1598

My soon-to-be boyfriend followed me to Italy. From my drawings it
was obvious I felt uncertain but excited by the prospect of his arrival.

I found a world of Jewish stories on church ceilings.

Finally, it was I who was living a miracle — the possibility of falling in love. After years of fear and fighting the feeling. There I was, a religious Jewish girl thinking about falling in love, as I drew New Testament scenes.

Pem
Vigi
† 4 Sa

Of course, when he arrived, I stopped drawing.
But my hopes and dreams were all over my pages.

On my return to London, a book on NYC arrived in NW3.

I wanted to study at a New York art school and complete my Master's there. But I recalled the screams and fights that occurred when my sister asserted her choices in life. Like the walls of the Red Sea after Moses departed, when Esther's rebellious spirit was absent the force of parental control overwhelmed me. I had the chance to take control, but I floundered.

Instead, I made another visit to New York, to a city I wasn't ready for, and to a boyfriend who wanted to build a relationship with me, when I was not even in a relationship with myself.

It is 2016 and I skype with FKC. She says, just because you write and draw about it doesn't mean you are over it.

My drawing enables my catharsis, but it is also a stick to beat myself with. Why was I such a fool? Why didn't I handle things more sensibly?

Instead of leaving my life behind, I carried my baggage with me for each visit.

He organised a studio and flat for me. I found a job in a gallery.
Yet I was waiting for permission to start my life.

Between the tailor and the drycleaner, just down the road from
the feminist bookstore. I didn't realise I needed to give myself that
permission, no one else could.

I made several visits. Such happiness and joy, interspersed by hysteria.

On the fourth floor of a Lower East Side walk-up, my life rose and fell.

A blistering hot summer of take-outs and outdoor cinema.

Perhaps my body knew what I could not cope with.
I always began my period on the flight home.

The fragility of our relationship was reflected in the frequent visits to the kiosk. So many flowers bought for neglected anniversaries, after arguments and breakups.

Within my possible freedom, I felt lost and trapped. All I could do was draw. A way to place myself in my new world.

My own mother cried into the chicken soup over my sister's romantic choices.

His mother had asked me 'is everything ok?' I remember the question but I simply had no words for expressing any distress, so I said I was fine.

I wish I'd known I could have found other mothers to talk to.

It is 2017 and I take Harry to the zoo on a sunny summer's day.
And I think about that time in New York.

I'd draw myself. I could have been anywhere.

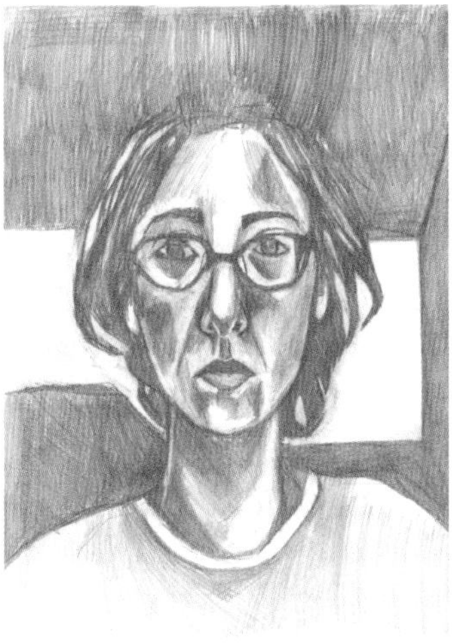
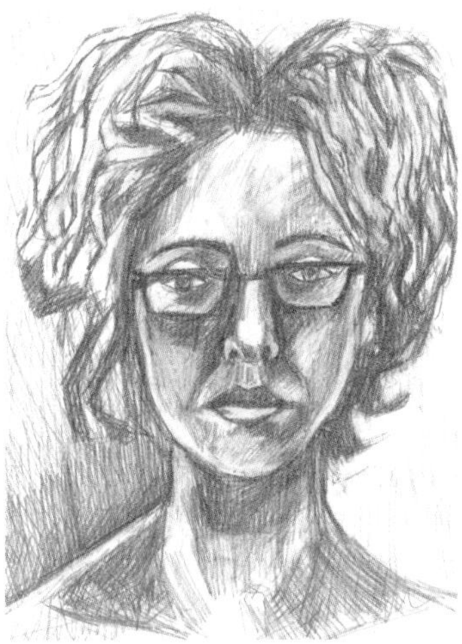
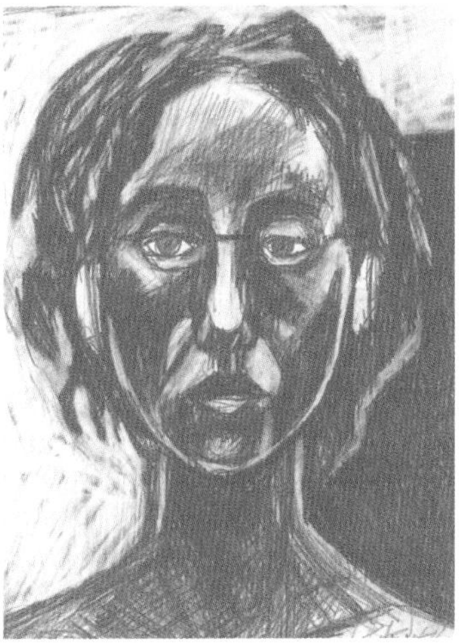
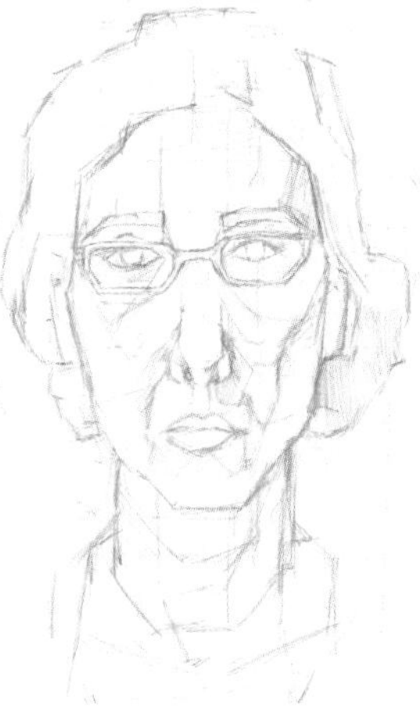
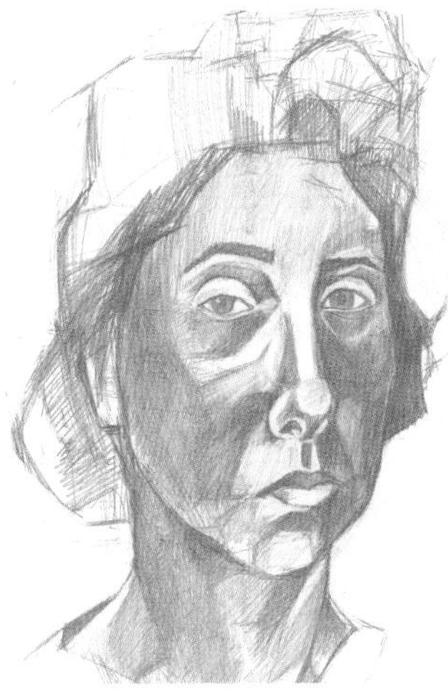
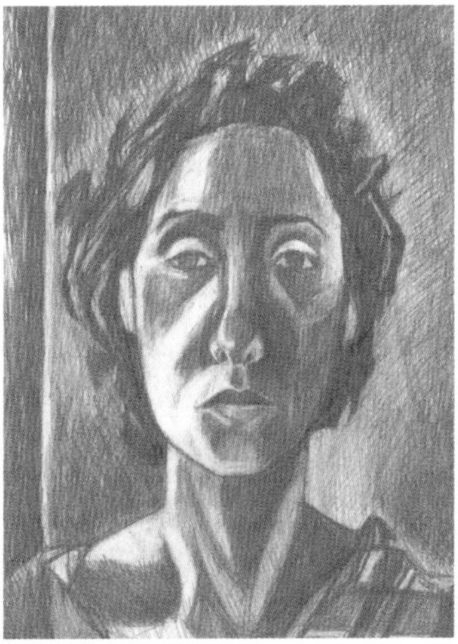
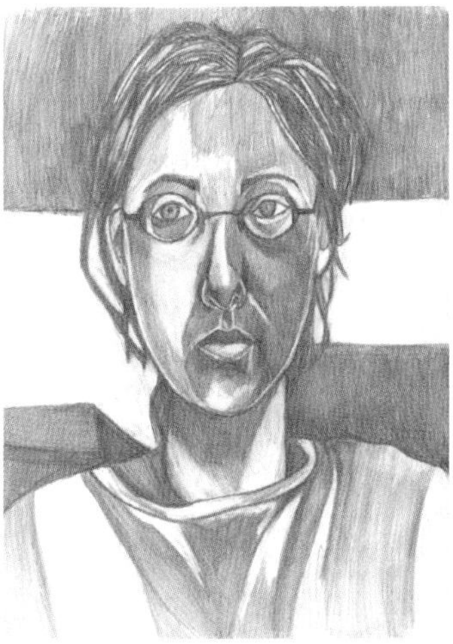
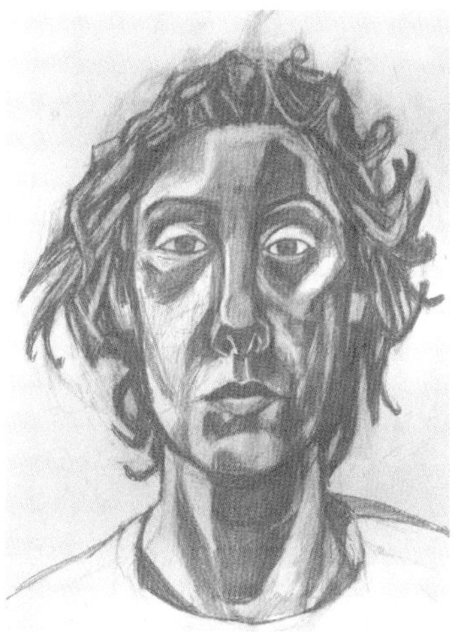
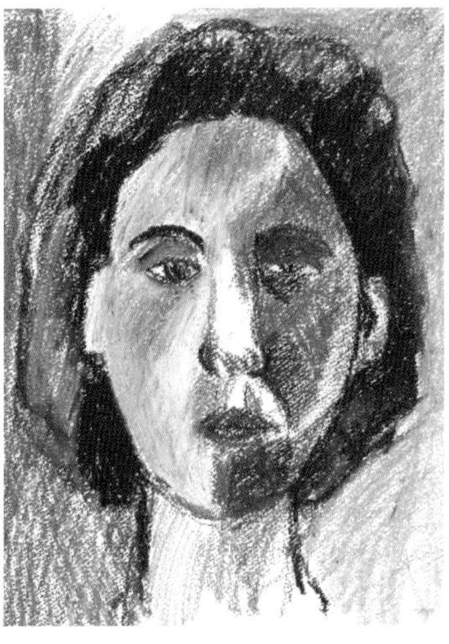

Ethics of the (Grand) Mothers:
Daphne, daughter of Esther, would say:
'You'll pine for us if you go to New York.'

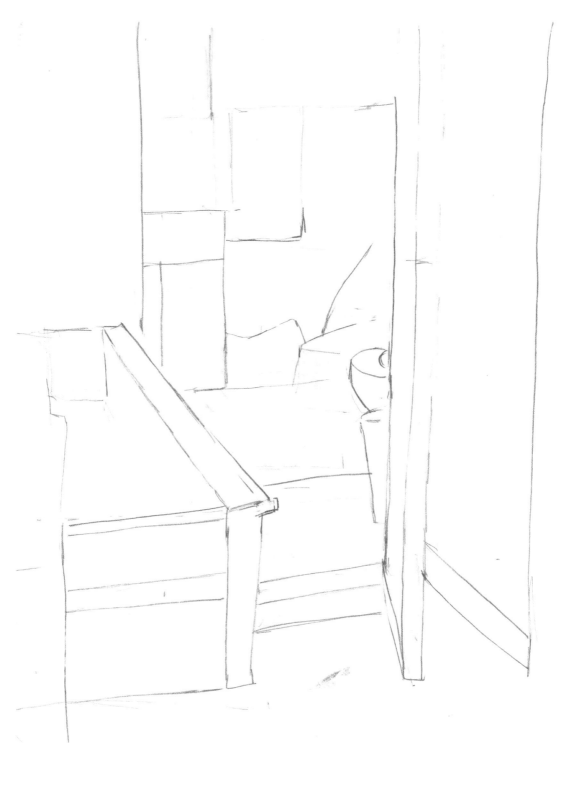

Each day, I'd tidy the flat, and swim and draw.
Clean, draw, cry. Claw, draw, cry.
Psalm 1999. By the waters of the Hudson River.
I painted. I drew and I cried.

The dog from the flat next door would cry and whine.
I never met the dog but we were soulmates. Lonely and lost
in the big city.

Did my grandmother predict, expect or demand this?

Highgate, 2016: my therapist suggests back then I struggled with my attachment anxieties.

'If you let her her go to America, I will divorce you', my mother had told my father. (I've already decided Harry can go anywhere, when the time comes.)

You should know there is a history of parental intervention in my family. My mother's father initially stopped her going to Oxford University. My paternal grandfather stopped my father furthering his aspirations as an academic.

My relationship in New York struggled on. In 2001 I came for a
summer. I hoped we'd get engaged. The panacea for a life lost in
transition. Or a life yet to be lived. Or the only way I knew to escape
my parents? It was all over already. I just couldn't bear to see it.

My visa ran out and I returned home.
I cried for a year in my parents' house.

Years later I learnt that the neighbours
had heard me howling in Hampstead.

How does the city sit solitary, that was once full of people?
She weeps sore into the night, her tears are on her cheek.

I was diagnosed and medicated. After a year, and two hospital visits,
the tears ran out. The boyfriend was condemned. My parents were
saviours.

Showalter's words, read in 2013, resonated: 'The dramatized female
plots... demonstrated that the signs and symptoms of schizophrenia
could be caused by the patient's unlivable situation in the home, as
the parents (but more often the mother) contradicted and fought their
daughter's efforts to achieve independence and autonomy.'

DEVASTATION

IS

A

PLACE

I

DON'T

WANT TO

RETURN

TO.

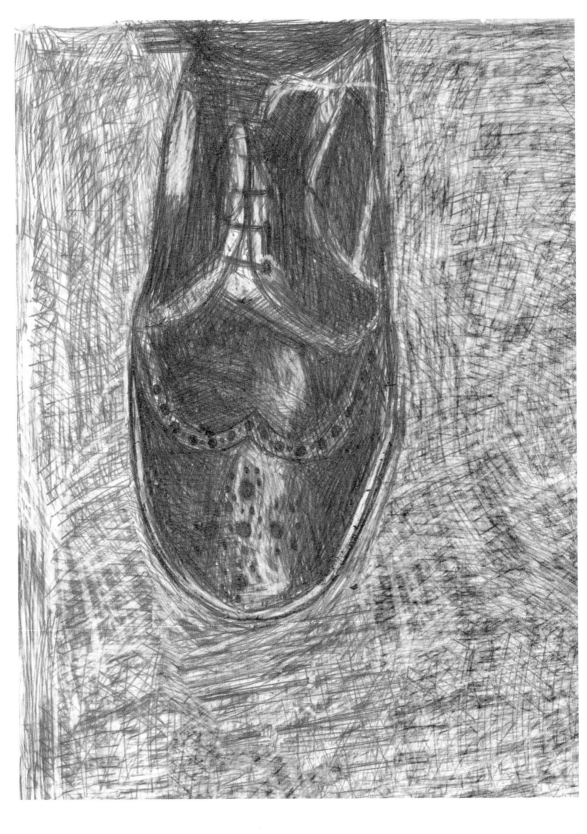

The therapist's shoes were shiny. He seemed sorted.
It made things worse.

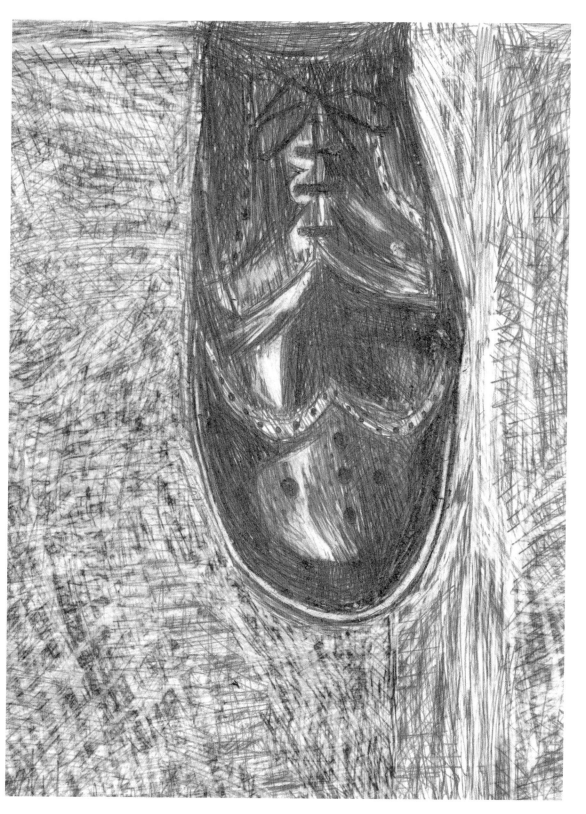

For my second beginning there was confusion and darkness over the earth. I said to myself I could either die right now, or start again. I chose life.

BAMIDBAR
MY WILDERNESS YEARS

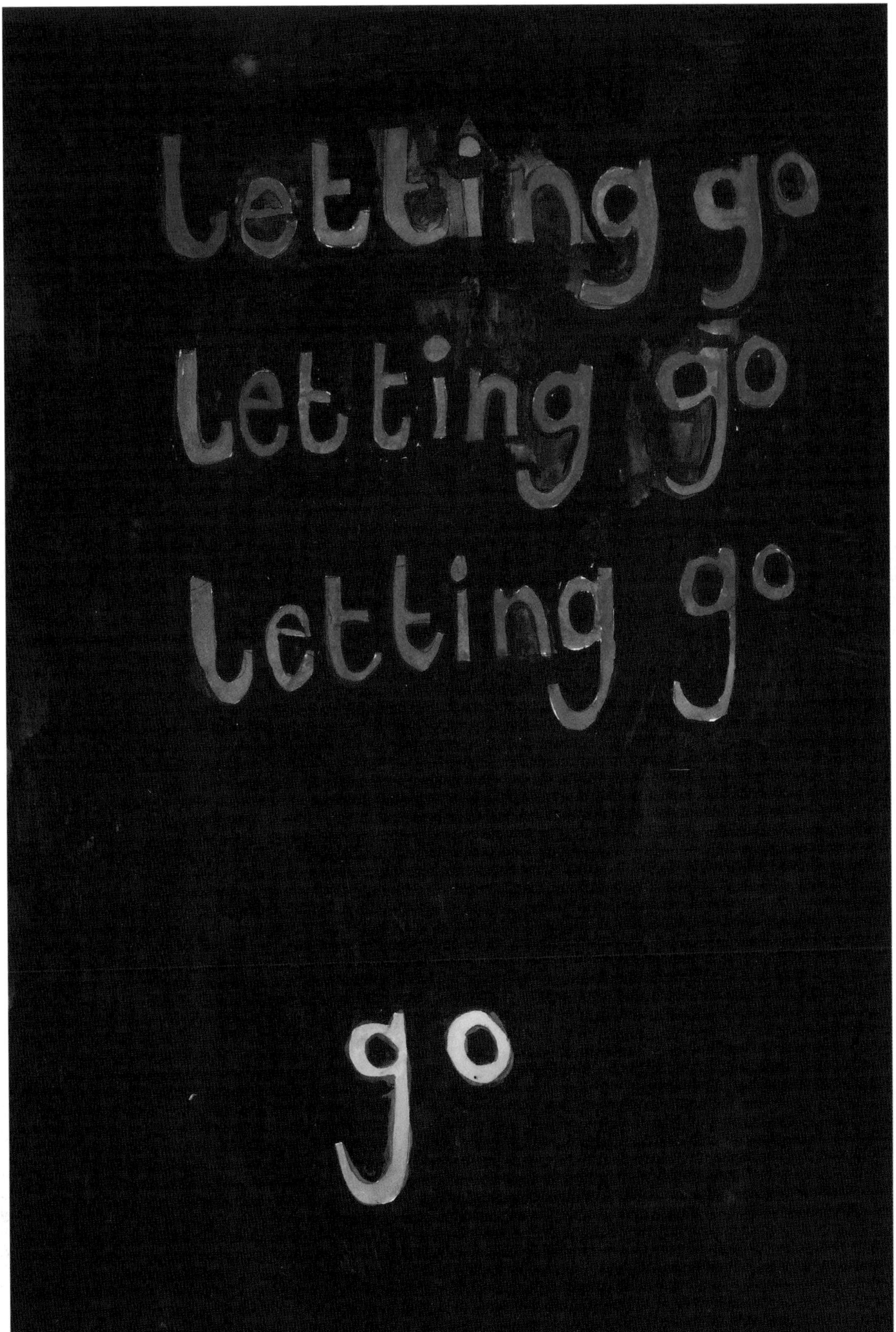
letting go
letting go
letting go
go

just
surviving
is
much more
impressive
than I had
previously
thought.

A Song of Descents and Ascents

2001-2012

She that goes
forth weeping
bearing precious
seeds doubtless returns
with rejoicing bringing
her sheaves with her

I was achingly aware of the trajectories of everyone else's life.
People were having babies. In Hendon, Netanya and on the pages
of da Vinci's drawings.

I applied for a job in Woolworths and was rejected. I worked
in shoe shops and sold decorative mirrors. I made future
promises that I didn't have to change for anyone.

I was set up on a blind date and wore unflattering red velvet trousers. After a stilted conversation at the Selfridges bar, he drove me home and, when I went to the bathroom, he promptly asked my flatmate for a date.

Days spent in regret.

You fool, you lost him.

Maybe it was a journey I had to take.

Everyone cries once a day.

Tentative hope. Plenty more fish.

I curated some art shows, sold a few drawings, but inside, the scaffolding of self was barely holding up. I was not established, ready or secure in the face of criticism, or disappointment.

The role of the good daughter/granddaughter came easily.
I was praised. Encouraged. The message I heard was that
another boyfriend would fix me and this hole inside. I put
aside struggling to be me in the world.

I made tea for my grandparents in my flat. There's a good feeling in making things beautiful for others to enjoy

I had a new teapot just for the occasion, it was a tea for them for all the teas they had made for me.

Afterwards I picked off the icing from my chocolate cake and placed it in the cake tin from my parents kitchen.

Memories stored for a future time.
We can never know when will be the final kiss goodbye.

From where I draw now, I can see a church and a synagogue.
Monuments to other people's capacity to believe.

I still believe good people get rewarded in their lifetimes. Special
people with no expectation or demands. People like Mrs Leahy.

When Mrs Leahy died, she had no family to clear her flat.
We three children were the children she never had and she
left us money. I used it to pay my PhD fees.

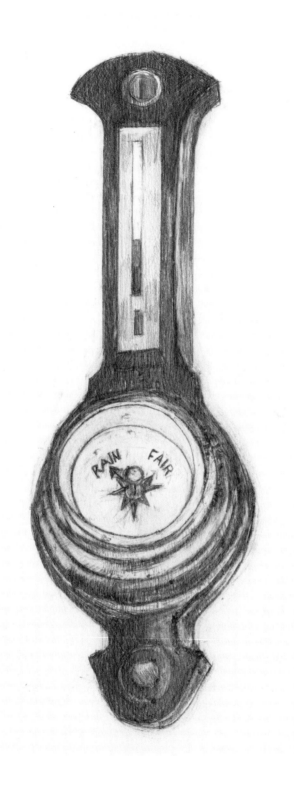

We cleared her flat, sharing out her possessions. I inherited the unpredictability of life and inevitability of a sad end.

Her mirror became mine. It had seen her face thousands of times.

I inherited lace from a great-great-aunt I never knew.
I am just a stitch in my family's intricately woven history.

Things and spaces speak for me.

In my parents' house there are all these books, Jewish books, bought in the height of my religious fervour. They stare back at me and tell me I should have married, had numerous children, and lived in a semi-detached house in Hendon or Finchley.

It was only in 2015, when he was nearly two years old, that my first, maybe only, child attended a synagogue service. Various members of the family are forever buying religious books for Harry.

Maybe I am a failed Orthodox Jew, or maybe I just grew up.
'What happened to you?' asked my youth group leader.

I don't know what to do with the books.
To keep or not to keep?

I'm reluctant to move them to our marital home.
I no longer need to chase that knowledge.

Harry and I read The Very Hungry Caterpillar and I
recall my numeric appetite as a single, insecure, woman.

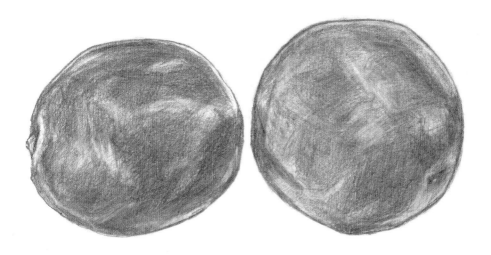

Two oranges when there were serious doubts about my PhD.

A jar of raisins when an article was pulled.

I say to myself 'by the time I've boiled a handful of pasta, someone will have emailed me'.

Two bananas when I thought my boyfriend no longer loved me.

Four squares of chocolate for lonely days.
A sickly sweet isolationism.

Oatcakes filled the silence when my friends didn't call.

I worked through a salad as I waited for a rejection from a gallery.

I had a friend for coffee and it became increasingly
clear she wasn't able to be supportive of my work.

Was it jealousy or ambivalence or general anxiety for me?

Afterwards, I felt sad, nostalgic for the days of uncomplicated friendship.

There was the promise of a romantic future in the gift of a plant.

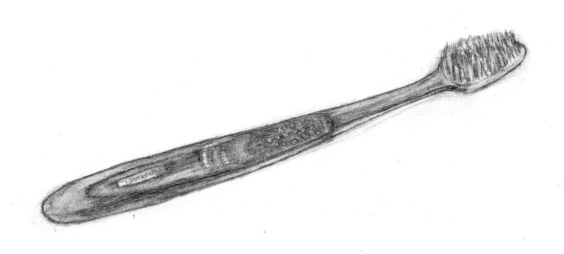

I had a toothbrush next to mine.

So did that mean I was your girlfriend?

17:00 06.02.

There followed a series of other men who never really loved me.

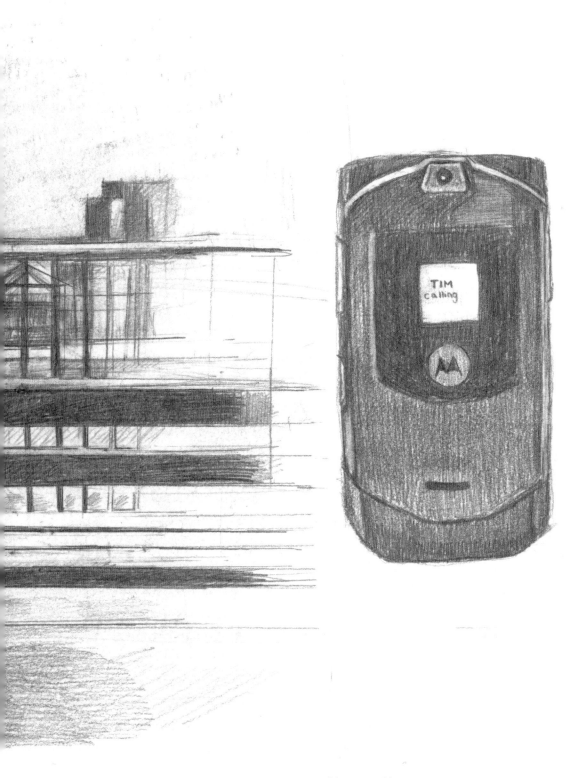

I sat on a bench waiting for him to call and tell me that he couldn't make it. It was fine, of course. I had half expected it.

Otherwise why would I have chosen such a comfortable bench with such a nice view?

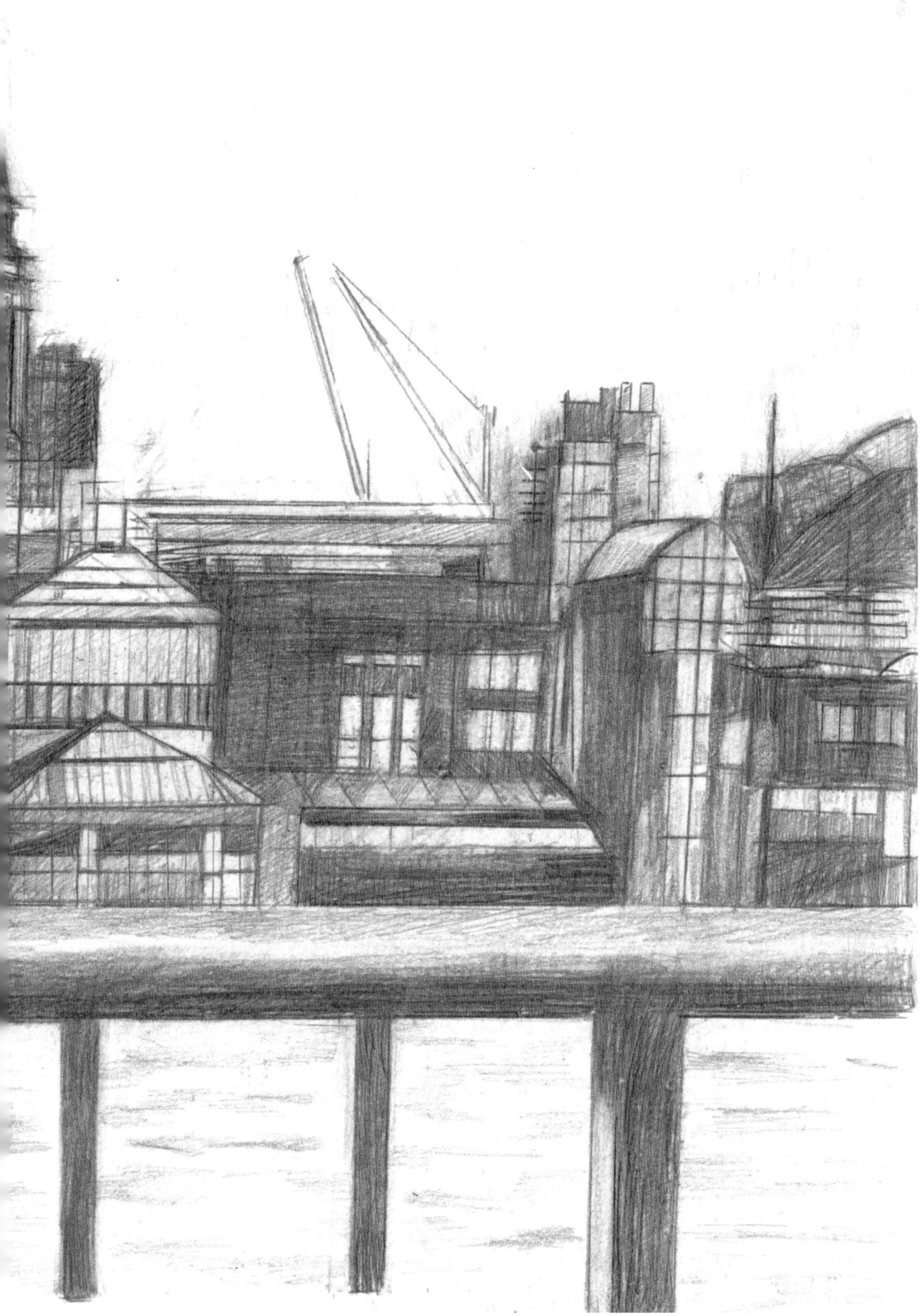

As I watched the water I knew you meant more
in your no-show than you cared to admit.

And that it was not just this afternoon I was going to spend on my own.

We had a lovely weekend
with birthday drinks and
a curry in Brick Lane.

I asked a stupid question
in a talk. I feel bad about
it now two hours later.

I am dreading the next
show I am curating.

Things improve. Only a
few times during the day
did I feel I couldn't cope.

I've been depressed and sad for three weeks. I just seem to walk around feeling terrible.

I feel somewhat better now. Not great but not overwhelmingly hopeless and disappointed.

He didn't call last night. In my heart I have stopped waiting.

I am on an upward curve. I feel slimmer and received a few encouraging emails.

I had a love affair with a friend of a friend.

I was happy while it lasted.

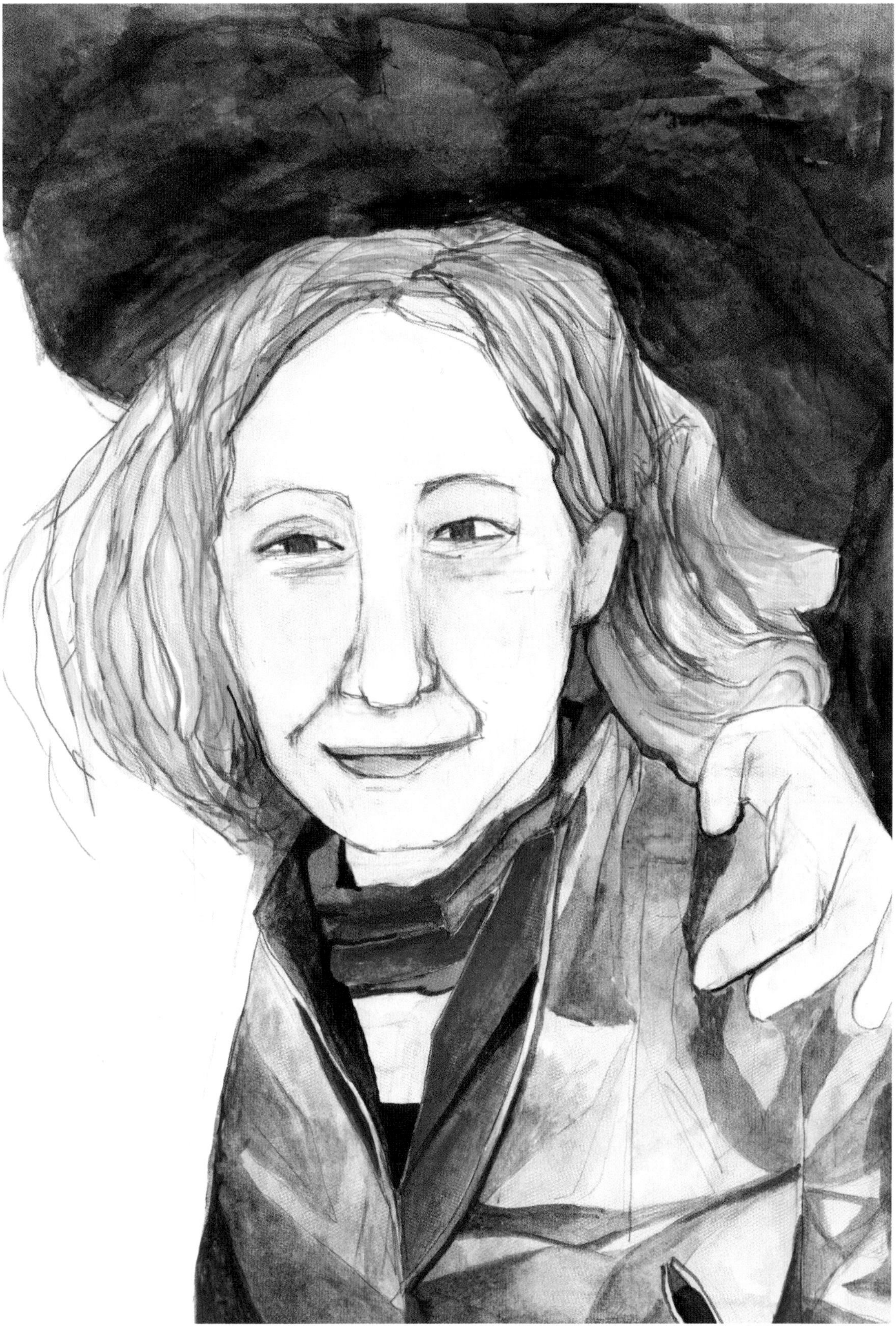

Happy with you.

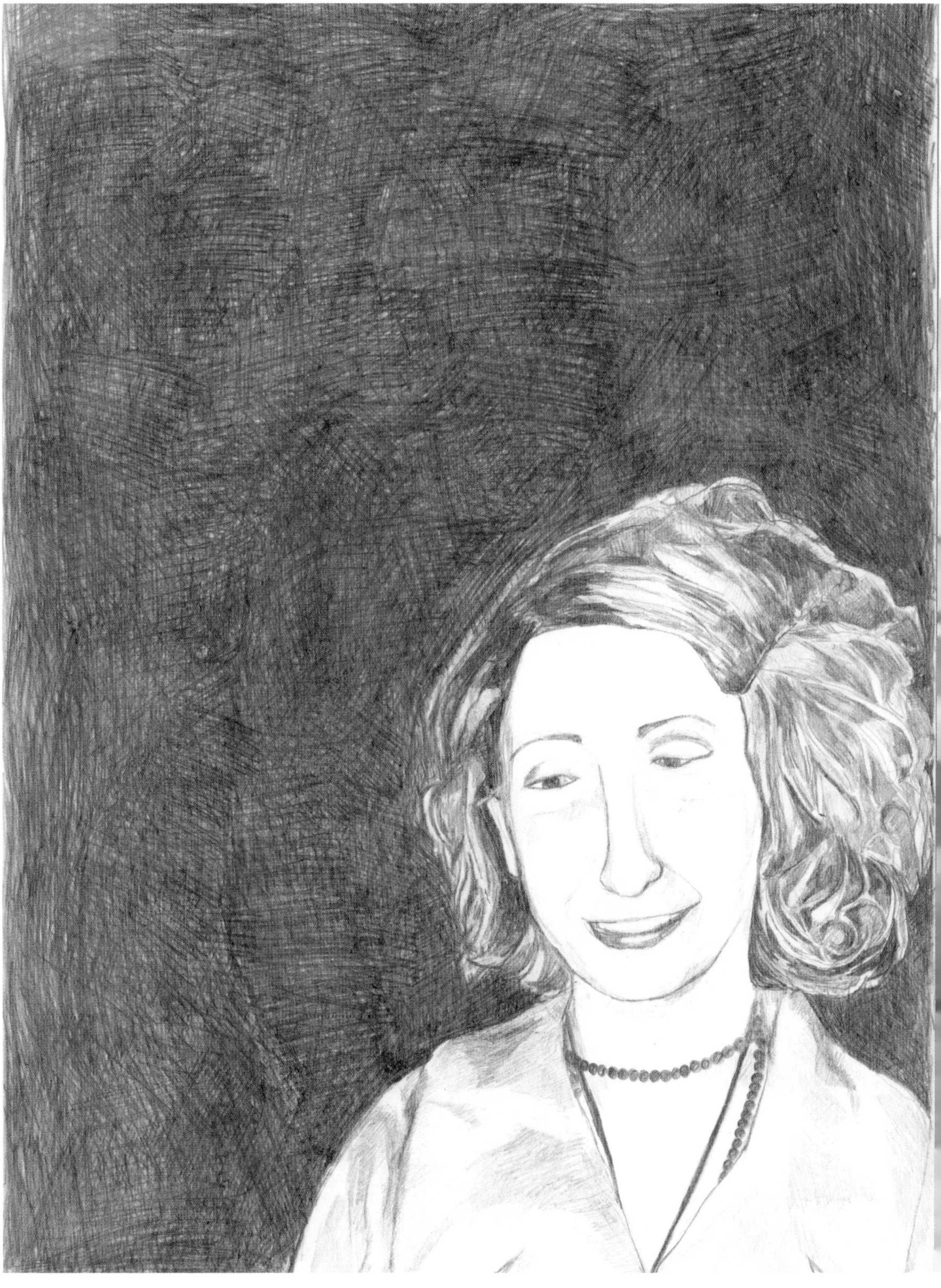

Happy now without you.

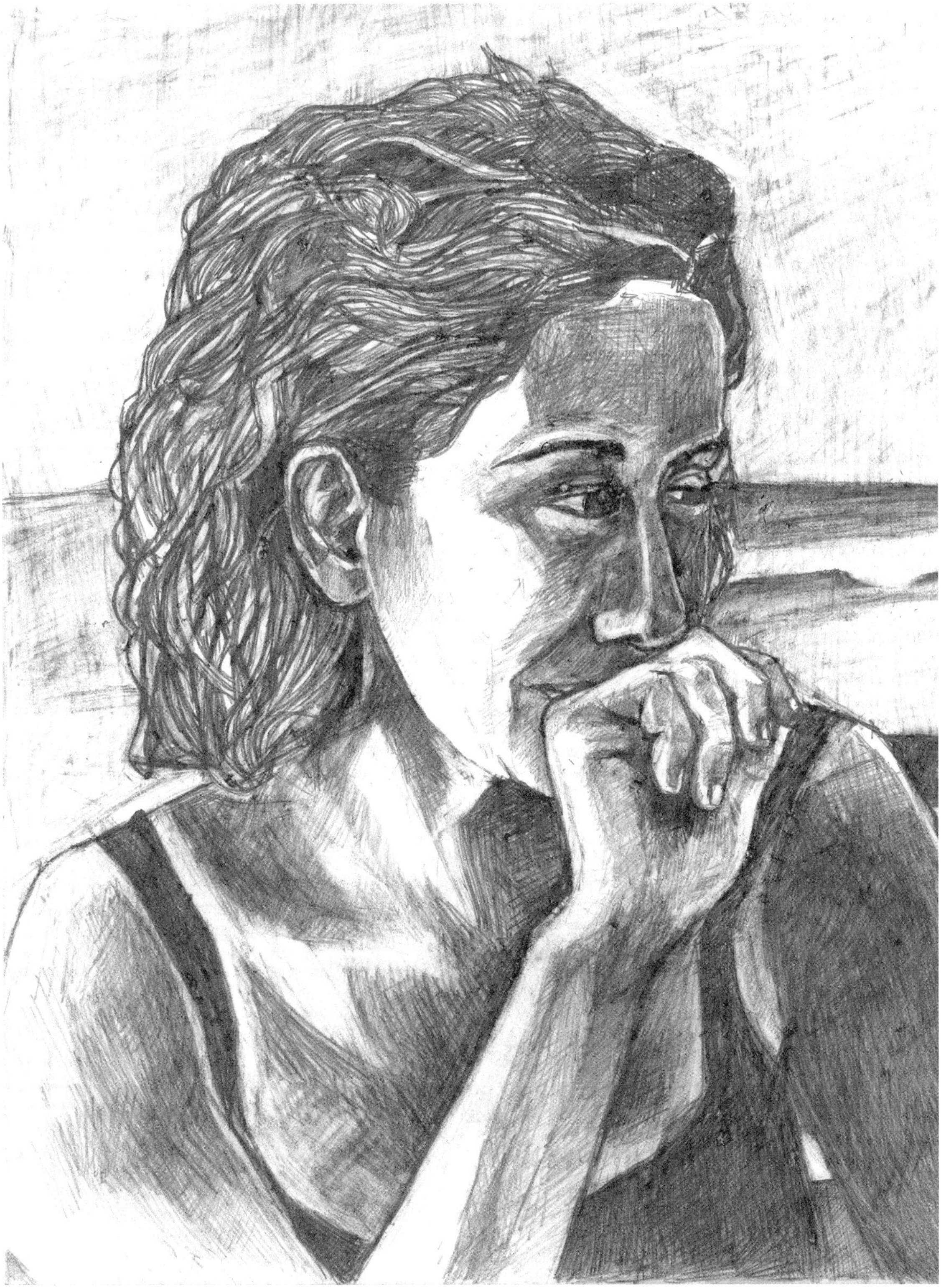

I'm mostly happy again.

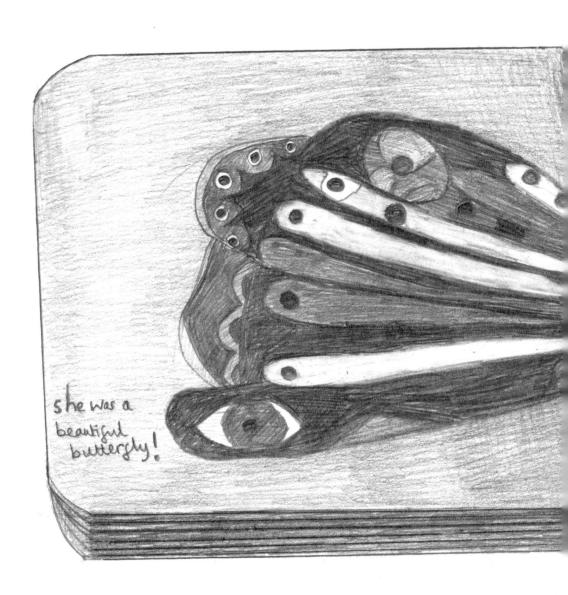

She was a
beautiful
butterfly!

I never did become a butterfly but in 2009 I found Charlie.

LEVITICUS
AND HE CALLED

In Mexico, I relaxed by the beach in my designer sunglasses.

Reading books on trauma and bereavement.

Such wonderful days.

I never wanted them to end.

Relaxed from my bleached hair to my sunburnt bunions.

Charlie waited till the last few hours of our holiday to propose.

Contrary to what it says on the tube of my moisturiser,
when he asked me to marry him I looked pretty rough.

You should know I really love Charlie. Just three months after our first date I flew to Australia to meet him on his travels. It was perfect.

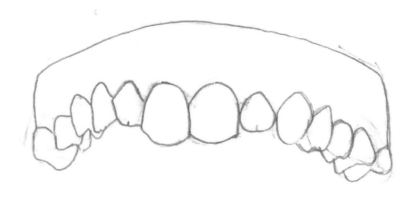

It's just the thought of a wedding that puts my newly whitened teeth on edge. I've hardly been happy since we got engaged.

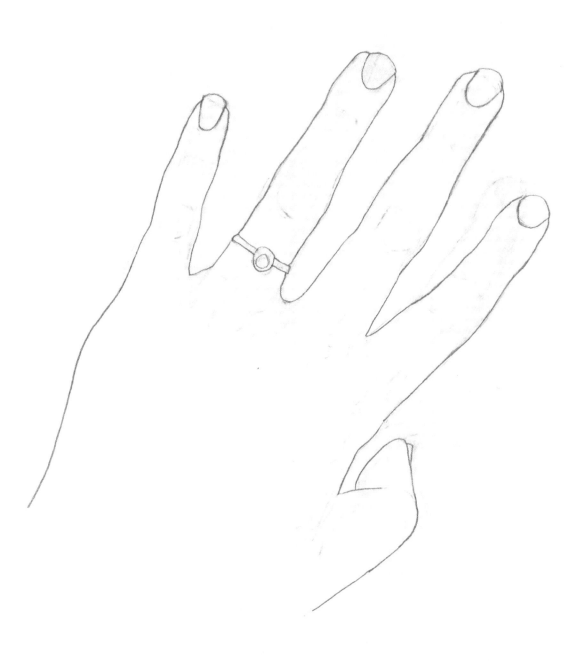

I could count the occasions I've worn my engagement
ring on one hand. Its value scares me.

As I said to my friends, it may not be the happiest day of my life, but it sure will be the most expensive. The woman selling me my tight white shoes was more excited than I was.

I bought a French lace bra for the honeymoon, but avoided adding matching knickers. What would my suffragette great-aunt think? How can I be a feminist in a traditional Jewish wedding?

Meanwhile my grandfather is ill and in hospital.

I visit every day and cry in the bath because he is in such pain.

9

Wards 9 N ✡ H

Vascular Studies

I am unconvinced of the benefits of medicine for a 92-year-old.

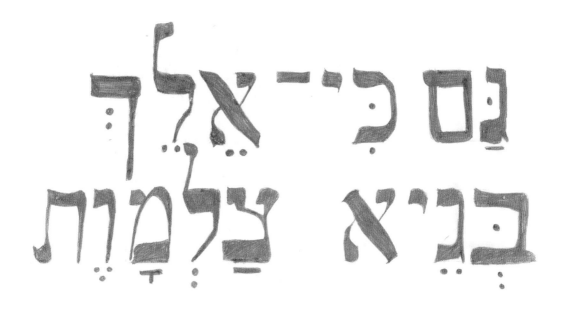

But still we visit every day and read him psalms.

This makes me glad and blessed to have a man I love who
will be my family now too. A candle for your Grandpa's
sweet soul, said the lady from The Burial Society.

2011-2012
SHANA
RISHONA
THE FIRST YEAR

If a man has recently married he must not be sent to war or have any duty laid on him. For one year he is to be free to stay at home and bring happiness to the wife he has married.   Deuteronomy 24:5

After our wedding, we did so much travelling. Two wandering Jews, looking for a home.

Finding clues for the next stage of our life.

I worried so much about losing myself in marriage. But I'm still feeling like me. Mistress of my destiny. My own personal epiphany occurred when I arrived back from honeymoon. And I realized just how happy I felt.

But still, something felt missing. Something I couldn't name. Did I need therapy again? I bought a self-help book on Amazon. Maybe it made a difference.

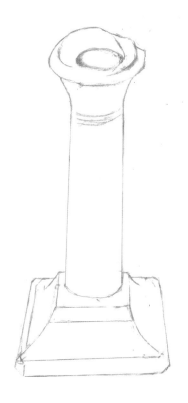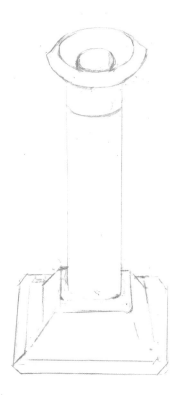

On Friday night in our flat we lit Shabbat candles in Grandma's silver candlesticks. They were from Pop on their first anniversary.

They were married for 62 years. The flat suddenly felt like home, and glowed all around us.

Thoughts of motherhood by an uncertain 36-year-old.

How long have I got left? Is it my choice any more? Was it ever?

My father said I shouldn't leave things too late.
My mother asked if I was having doubts.

One friend, unprompted, told me of her two-year struggle to have a child.

Another told me she was freezing her eggs to wait for Mr Right.

But when I talk all this through with Charlie, he said in his calm way that we weren't rushing things. I felt I loved him that little bit more and felt so glad he was by my side.

I tried to focus on self-care that doesn't revolve around food.
But I kept being drawn back to baking for other people. I must
have been filling a cake-shaped hole in my life.

My need to feed might just be thwarted maternal instinct.

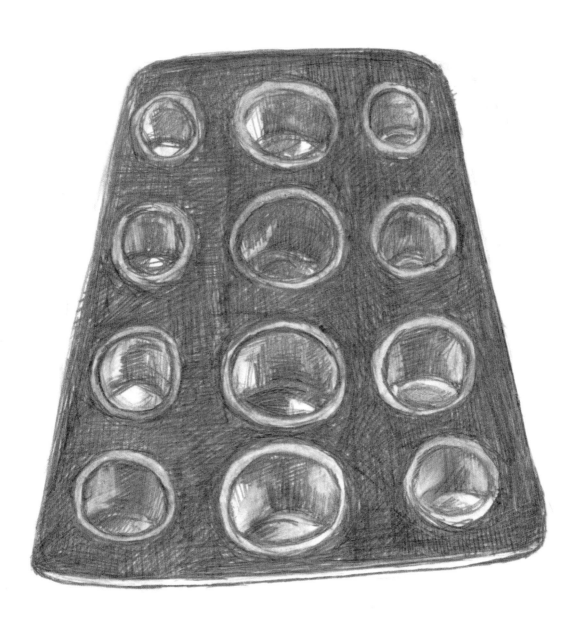

Back to that egg thing again.

I'm afraid of transitions in
my life. They are always
accompanied by a dark side.

The maths of life. A birth. A death.
A marriage. A death. Someone's
happiness. Someone else's tears.

Part of me can't wait for
this countdown to finish.

Part of me is terrified
of what happens after.

I haven't seen my grannies in weeks, so I went today. I am so pleased I did.

One granny predicted a girl, the other wants to knit some booties. Will you have your daddy's gentle nature? Is it too late to make a request?

I carry a heaviness within me. It wakes me at night. It kicks me in the morning.

Your little head pops out – a bump in my side. Then pops back in again. Hallo, baby. Hallo little blessing.

HARRY'S GENESIS

My son is five days old. Yellow, loud and hungry.

Smile, said the midwife.

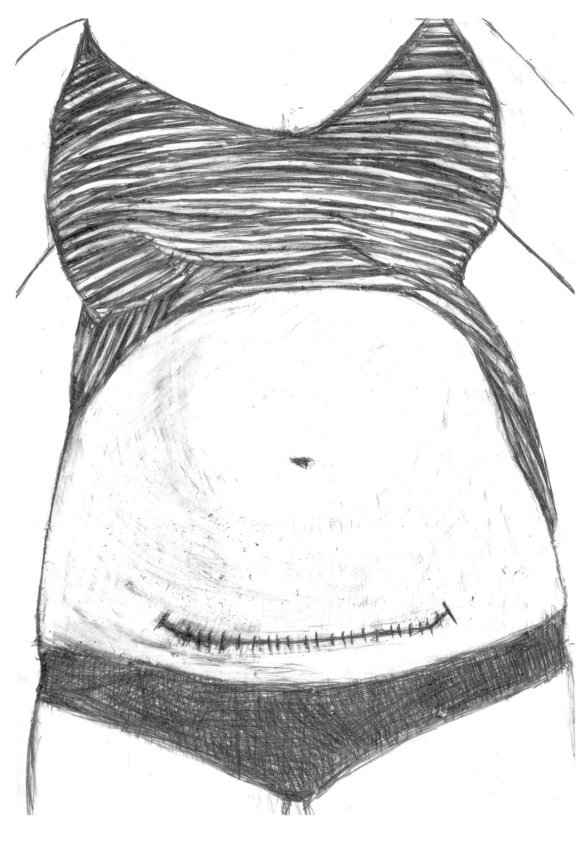

You have a beautiful scar.

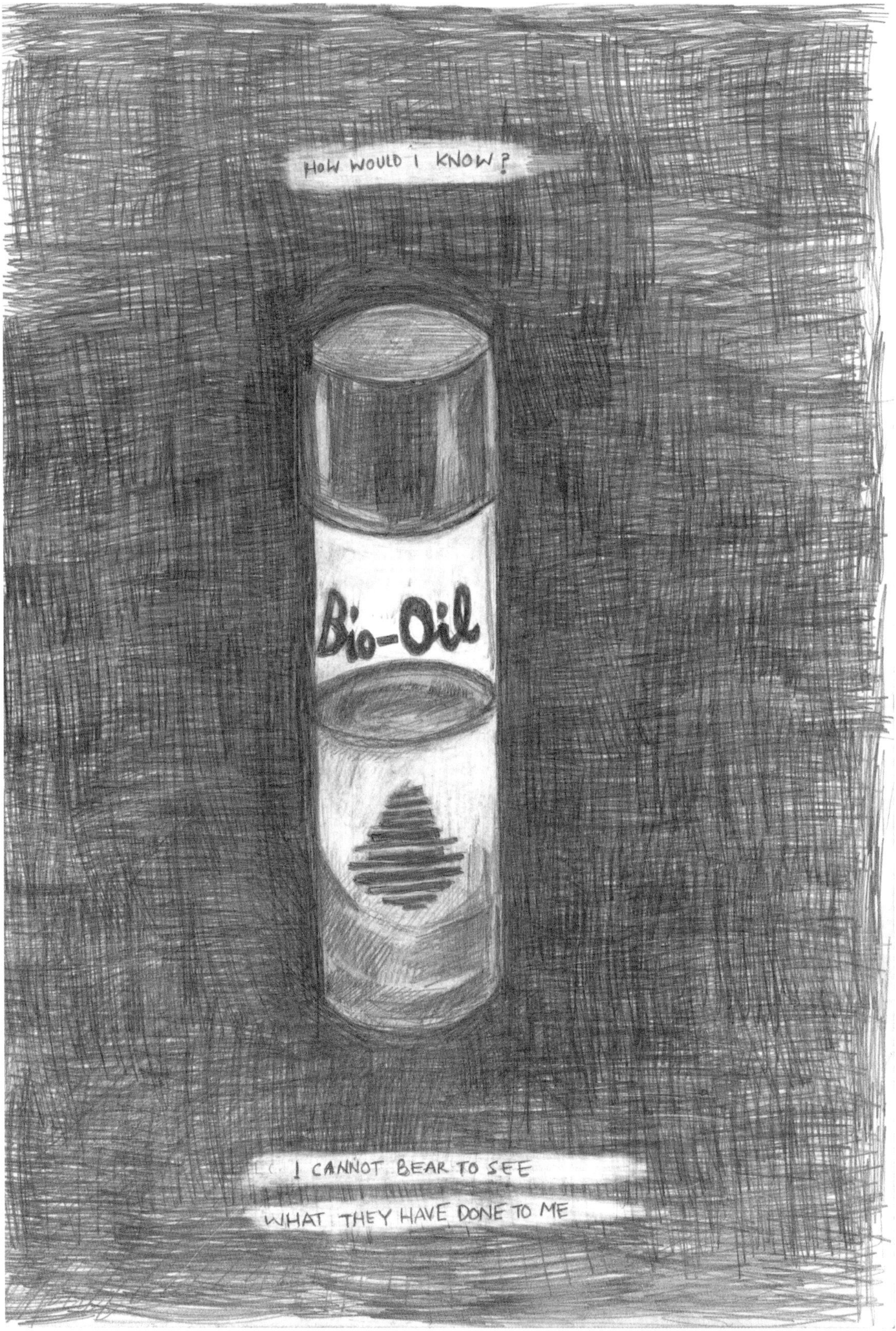
HOW WOULD I KNOW?
Bio-Oil
I CANNOT BEAR TO SEE
WHAT THEY HAVE DONE TO ME

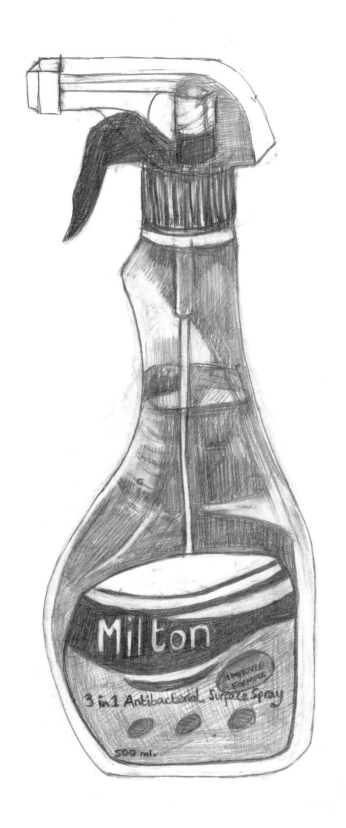

Tidy up, dry, repeat. Tidy up, dry, repeat.

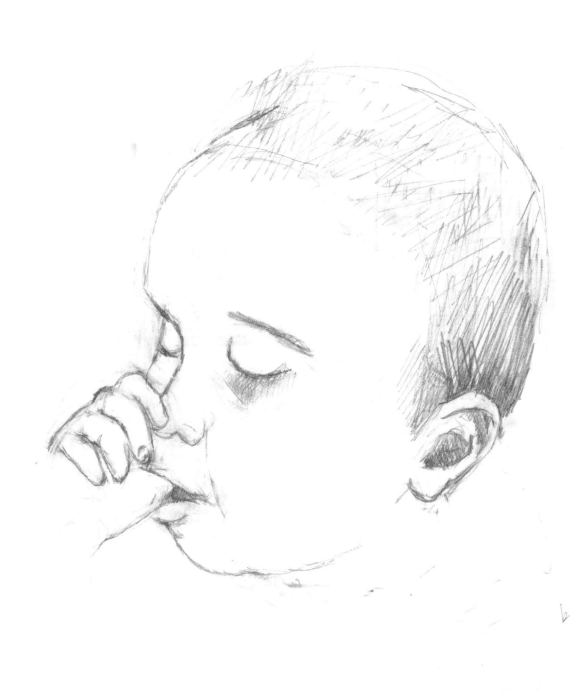

You sleep. I can hardly move for tiredness.

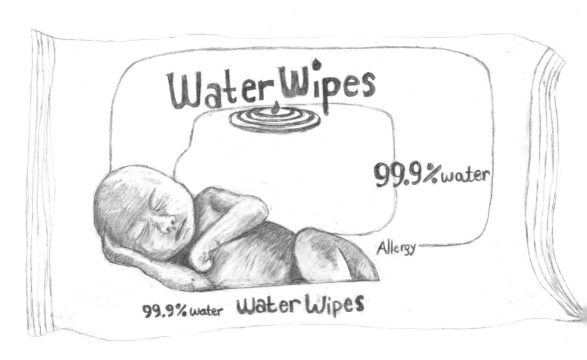

Wipe nose. Wipe bottom. Repeat, repeat, repeat.

Over three weeks old. Loud, beautiful, always hungry. Circumcised.
Named. Loved. Centre of my world. Clock of my day. Master of the
household. My breasts ache for him. My belly lonesome.

My aching breasts, your happy face.

The nanny saves me, I pay her. Yet she steals your first laugh.

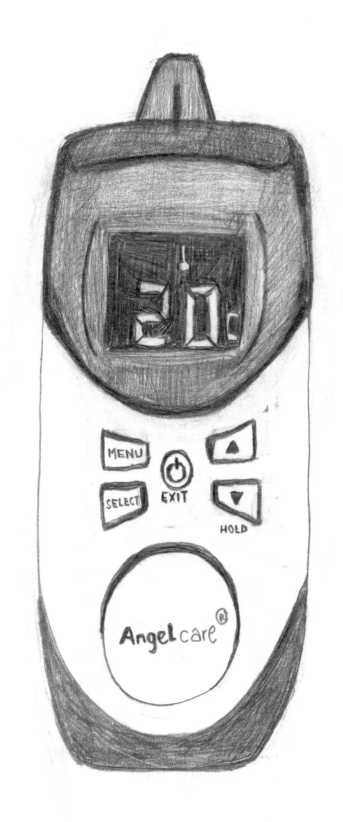

My nights – a series of your most determined interruptions.

Oh, my little love.

My breasts make me a slave to my son. I went to swim, but he howled in my absence.

I cannot have a full day alone. I am trapped.

I love his eager smile and laughs of joy at feeding time. I feel so incredibly popular.

My breasts ache for him, wait for him. I walk out of the shower dripping with milk. I am already a mess before I have even got dressed.

Six months old. We planted a cherry tree.
Surrounded by your mummy, daddy and all your
grandparents, we fed you pureed carrot. (You spat it out.)

Ethics of the Grandmothers:
Gwen, daughter of Golda, wife of Harold, used to say:
'No flies on you'.

Three months before she died, she said:
'I'll be watching you from a telescope from Heaven.'

Nine months before Grandma died was Harry's first night.

He lay beside me, and as I tensed at his newborn uneven breathing,
I recalled prayers I hadn't said in a very long time.

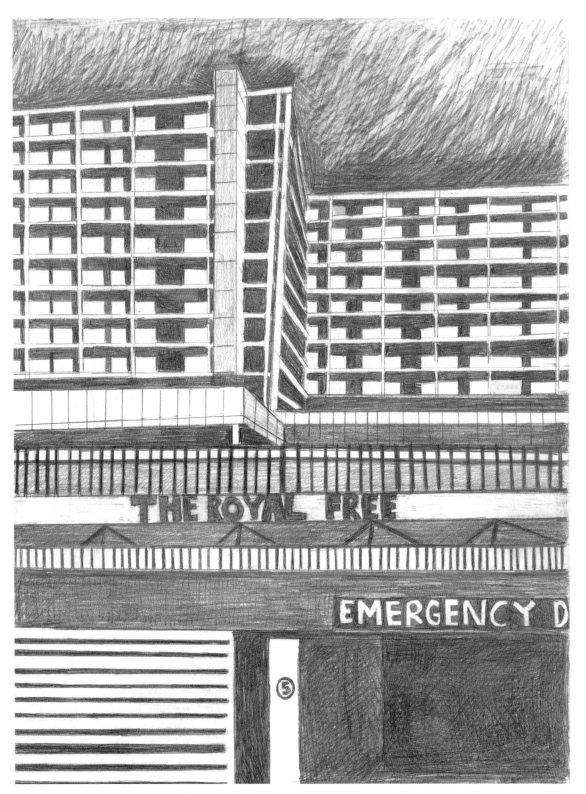

Grandma fell on a Saturday evening. There was a hard night in accident and emergency. She was moved to the chaotic geriatric ward where my grandfather had died 18 months before. I recognised the exhausted nurses and they recognised me.

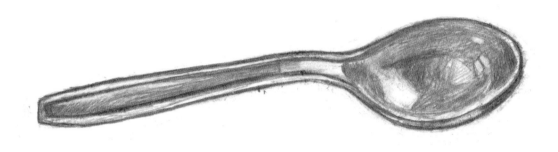

Grandma was confused in hospital. After she was released she still
did not eat properly. We would visit her at the home and gently spoon
orange juice into her mouth. I returned home to feed Harry purees.

I bought her favourite biscuits from our nearby Tesco. Grandma would take small bites, then place the biscuits on the table. And always say 'Genuk is Genuk': Enough is Enough.

The last time that I saw Grandma she had shrunk to a
tiny figure. She cupped her hands around my face, looked
me in the eyes. 'I love you,' she said to me without words.

'Poor Old Fox has lost his socks' is Harry's favourite lift-the-flap book. My dad seems to forget things more often these days. One buggy. One wheelchair.

Friday night is Shabbat and Harry grasps his prayer book.
And on Monday, Tuesday, too. An uncomplicated love for the
day of rest and religious rituals. 'Shabby Shabby' he calls it.

Throughout the memorial evening for my Grandma,
Harry plays with his yellow bus in the centre of the
room. Life with death. It's easier that way, isn't it?

Every day, I am a knife-edge away from fucked-up motherhood.
One grape, one door hinge, one plug socket and it's a disaster.
All the accidents that Harry might have.

Every day, Harry goes for a walk with the nanny, and
brings me back a gift, a leaf, a flower. I collect them as
relics of his love, of times when I was an absent mother.

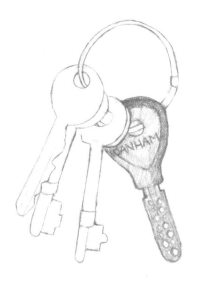

Harry loves keys. And
comes into my office.
And tries to open the
garden door.

An apple collected
from our garden.
Thank you, Harry.
And thank you for
the others, too.

REVELATIONS

We are one. He is one.
And I am a year a mother.
The sun shines in the December sky.
I walk him round to my parents' house. He brings them light.
I push him on the swings, to the sound of his laughter.

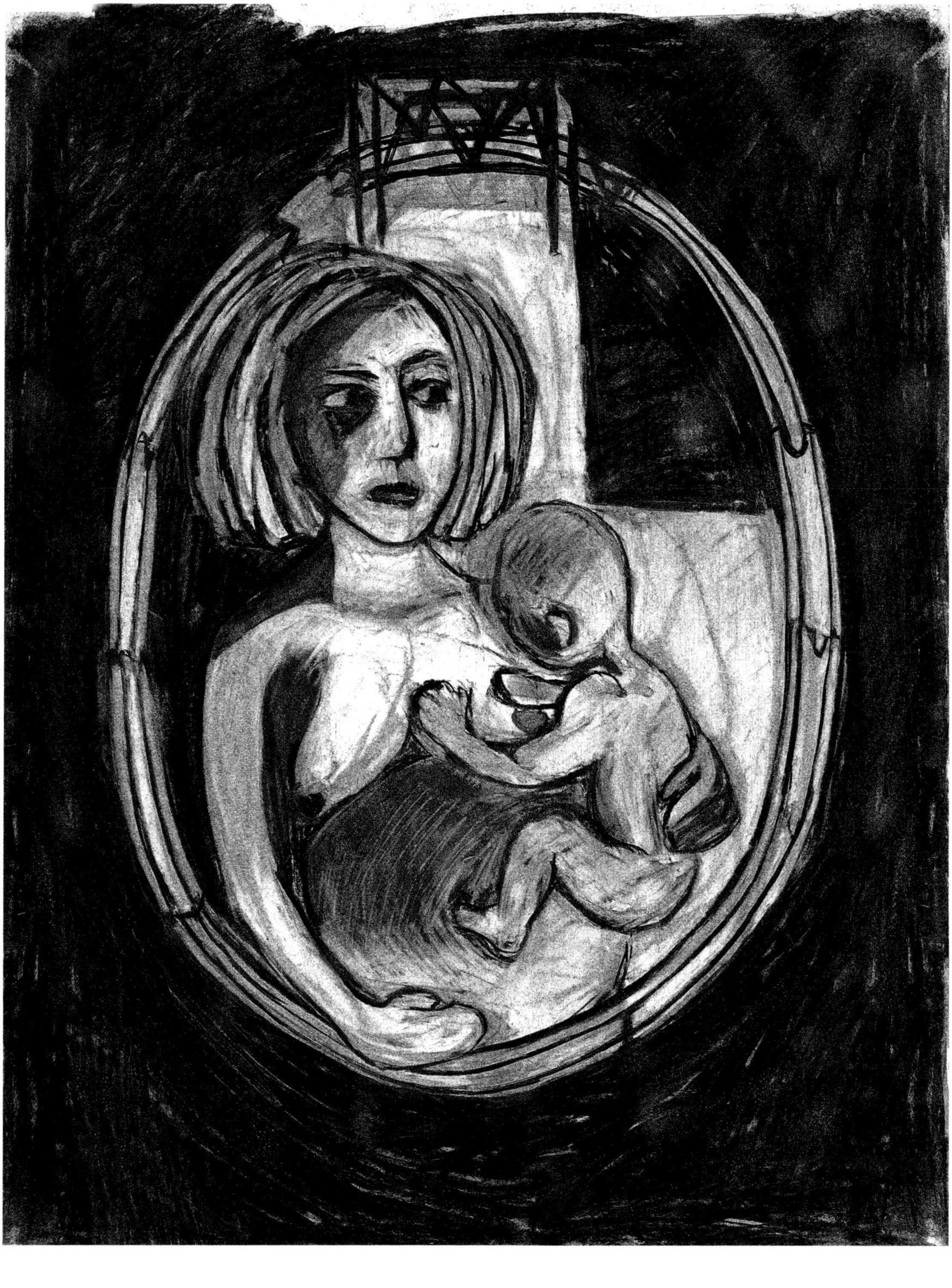

It could have ended here.
It would have been nice. A poetic circle.
And yet. I woke up one morning in 2015 and I
couldn't bear my life. Swings and roundabouts?
But I wanted to get off.

Therapy. Individuation. Understanding my family.

Realising I was not responsible for anyone's happiness: I don't
need to be anyone's good girl or daughter or granddaughter, even
wife. I was entitled to my life, to my own autonomy and dreams.

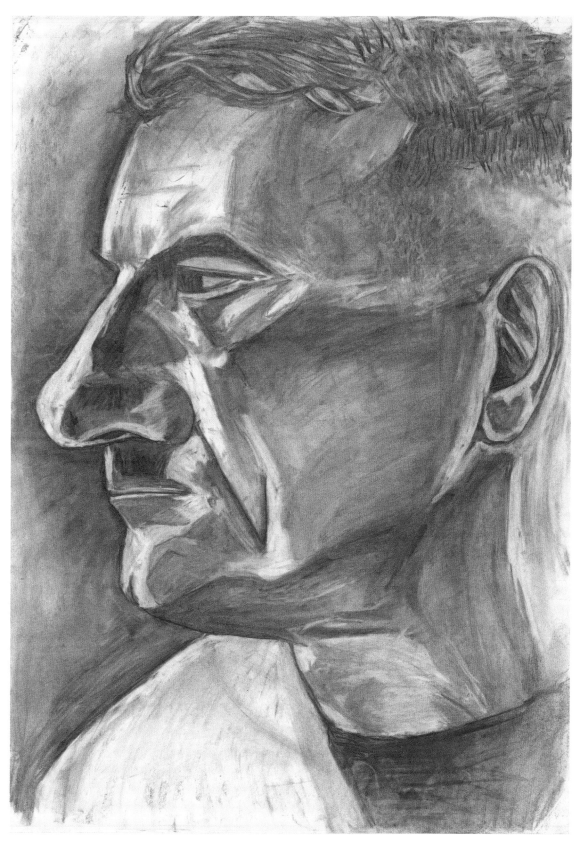

I'm here. It's better.

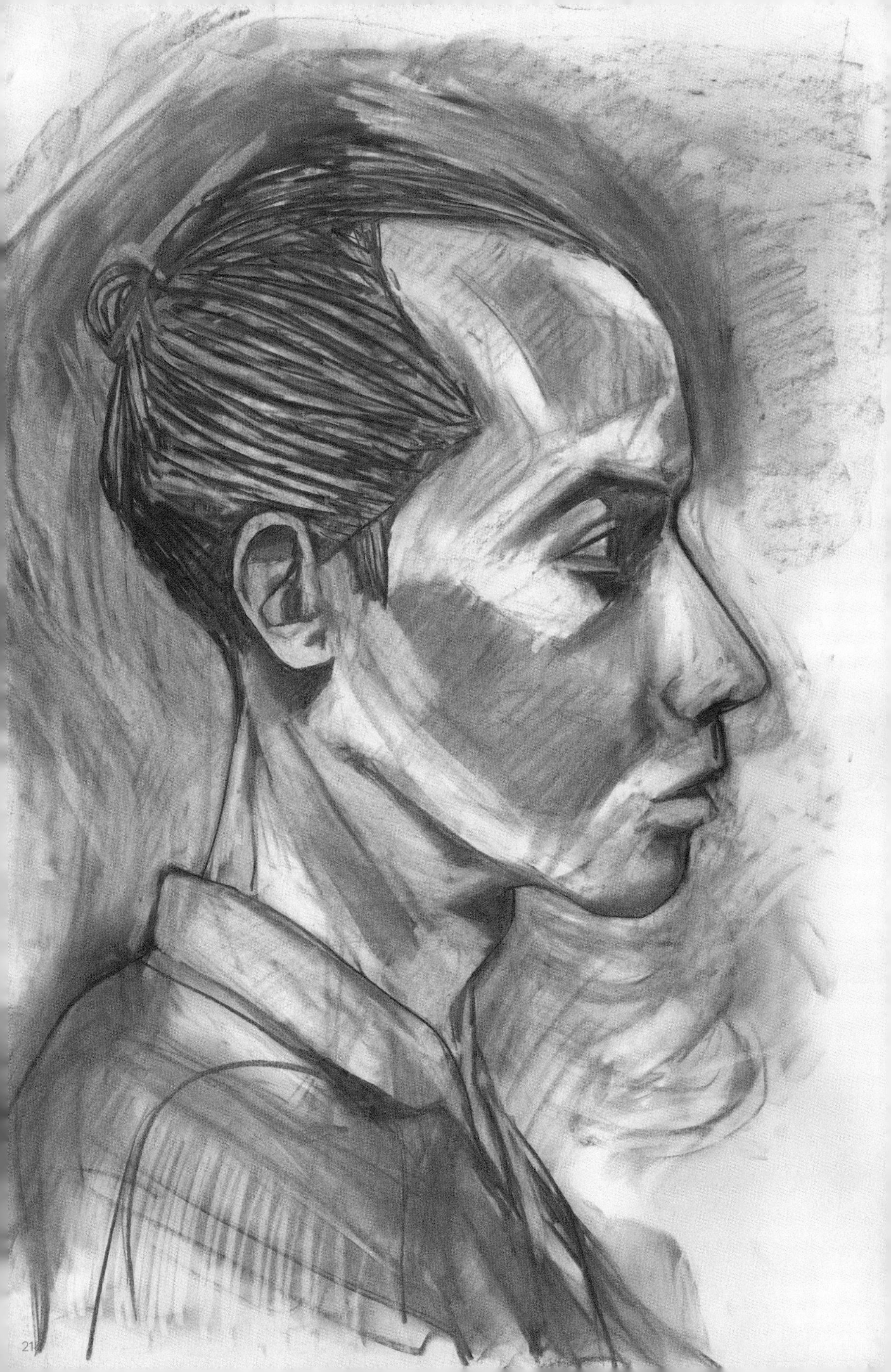

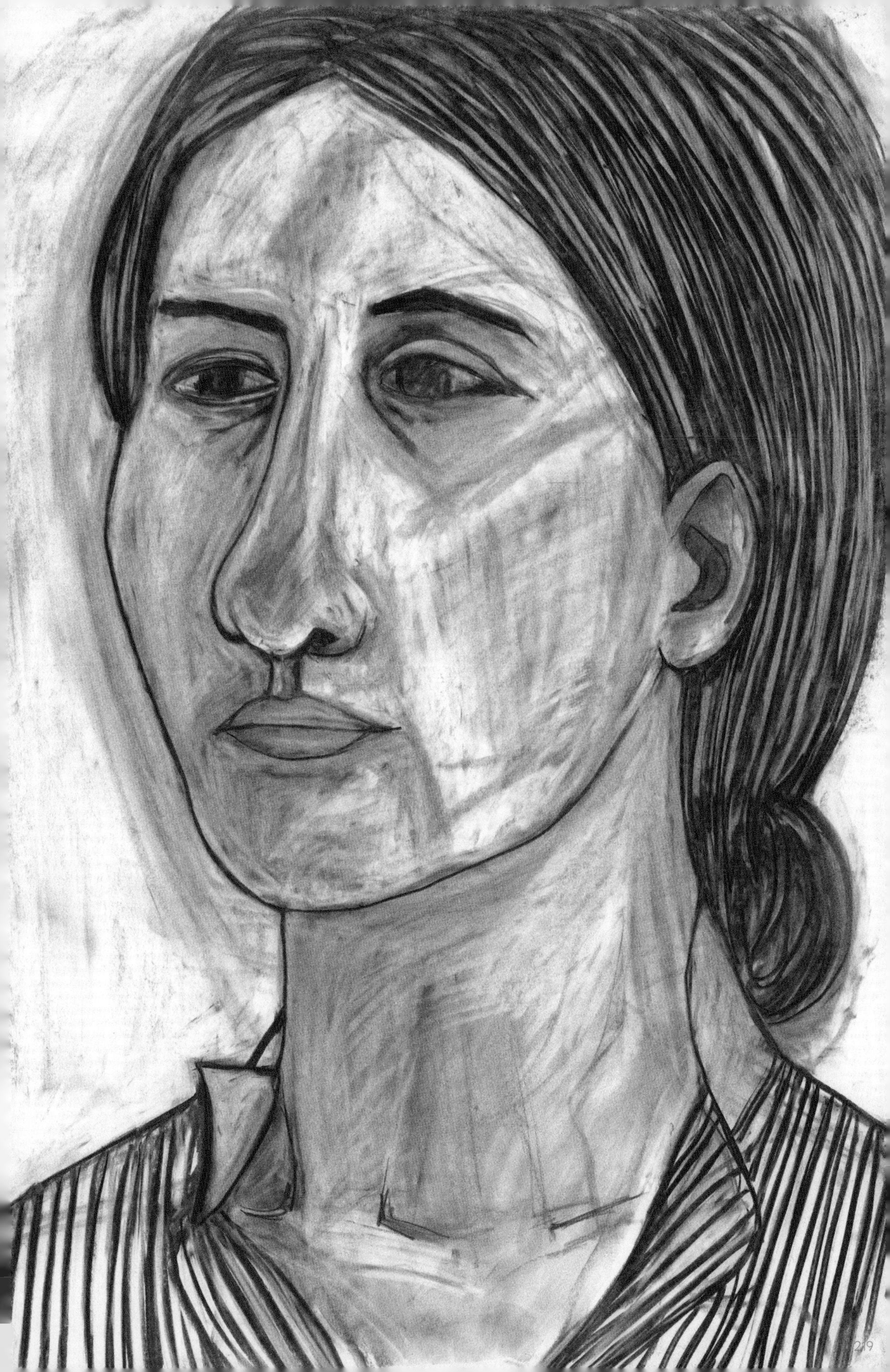

It was a Friday morning and I was on my way to therapy

and I delighted in the clear beauty of Parliament Hill.

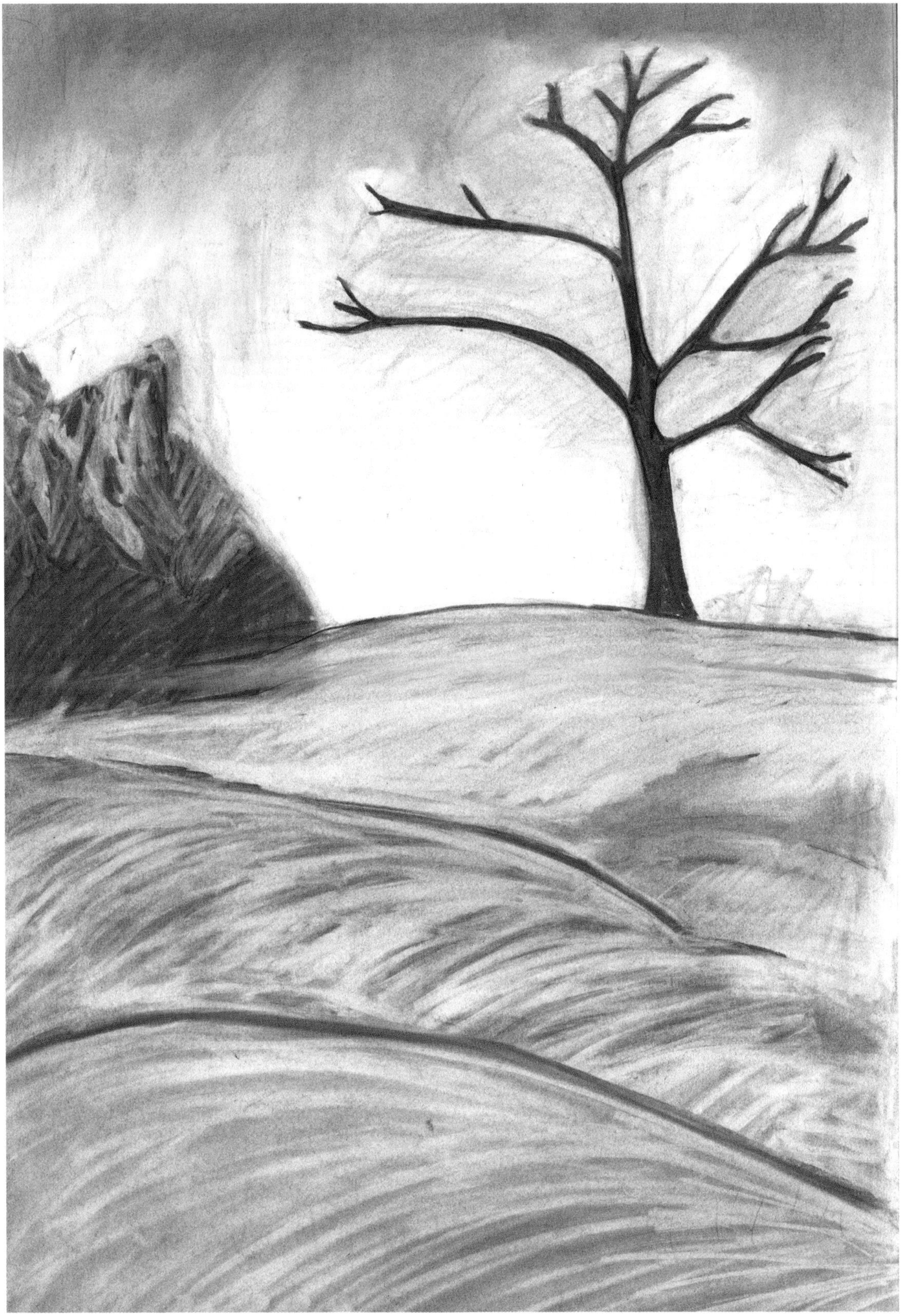

Not perfect. But better.

Started to paint again. Joined a Reform synagogue and attended regularly with Harry. Felt fury and frustration. Allowed myself to resent opportunities that were withheld from me, that I had withheld from myself.

I set up an artist salon. Finished my PhD. Got an art studio. Started life drawing. Stopped cooking dinner. Joined a beginners yoga class, and finally felt I had a space for me and my body to be one. Worked on my drawing. Stopped working on my drawing. More therapy. Talked about my feelings, and stopped just drawing them. Stopped asking art to solve all my problems and started solving them with actions. Found some friends just didn't fit anymore, so I let them go. Made new friends. Made art a job not a bandage. Felt angry, angry, angry at people. But mostly angry at myself.

And very sad. Because a nice drawing is not a life lived and no salve for a life of unnecessary pain.

I won a grant to New York and took Harry for a month. Celebrated
Purim as a family on the Upper West Side. Charlie and I dressed as
builders and Harry as Super Grover.

Wished I'd been this capable and confident years before. Felt as alive
in the city as I ever had. Felt devastated not to live here. Realised how
near I was years ago and what support I needed then to grow. But
back then I didn't even know how to ask for help. This time I had
transnational therapy on Skype at Borders on Broadway.

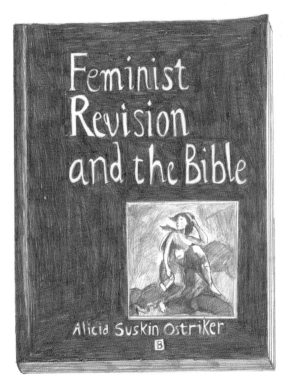

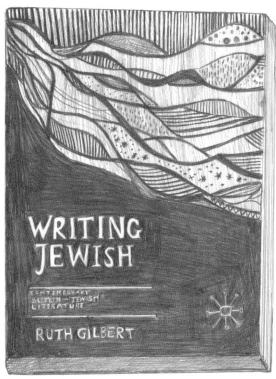

I found feminist Jewish theology and writings.

I heard my voice amongst other women's voices.

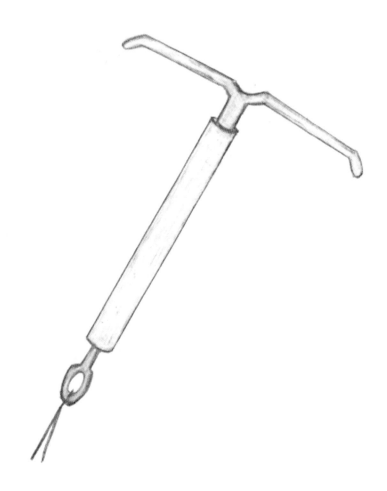

I booked a doctor's appointment, without telling my husband.
I had a coil fitted and decided I would have no more children.
I would now focus on me.

But it hits me every day. The pain of realising I never felt for
my first 42 years that I could be the driver of my own life.

My therapist suggests it was never a given
that I would even get to this stage.

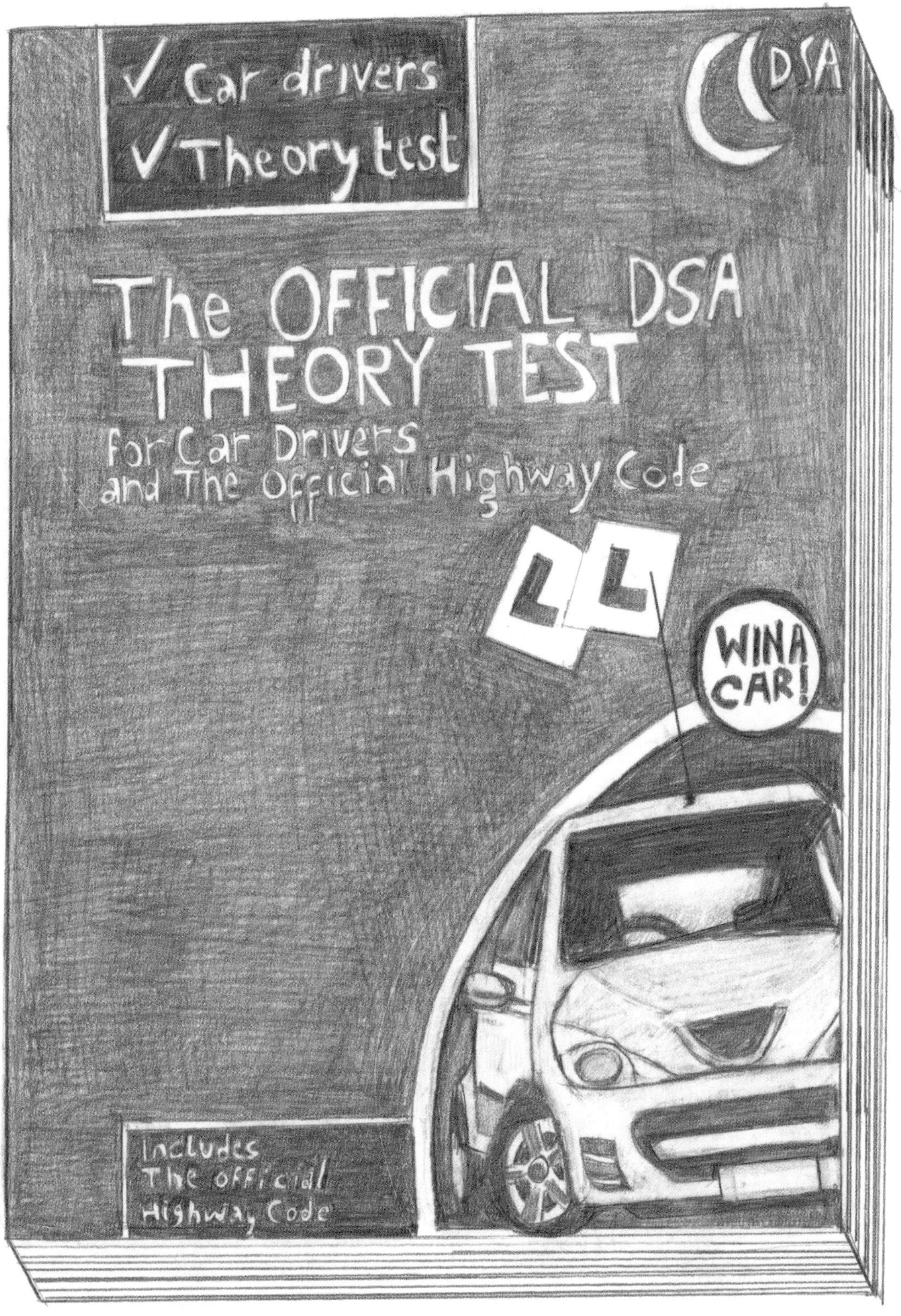
✓ Car drivers
✓ Theory test
DSA
The OFFICIAL DSA
THEORY TEST
For Car Drivers
and The Official Highway Code
WIN A
CAR!
Includes
The official
Highway Code

And I still can't drive.

Sarah, Sarah, come out of the shadows.
This is your life. This is your time.

But it's 8.30 am and I must first take my son to nursery, on the 46 bus.

Then, after that, I'll travel to my studio again.

My new canvases will have arrived and I'll make
a new self-portrait, in colour.

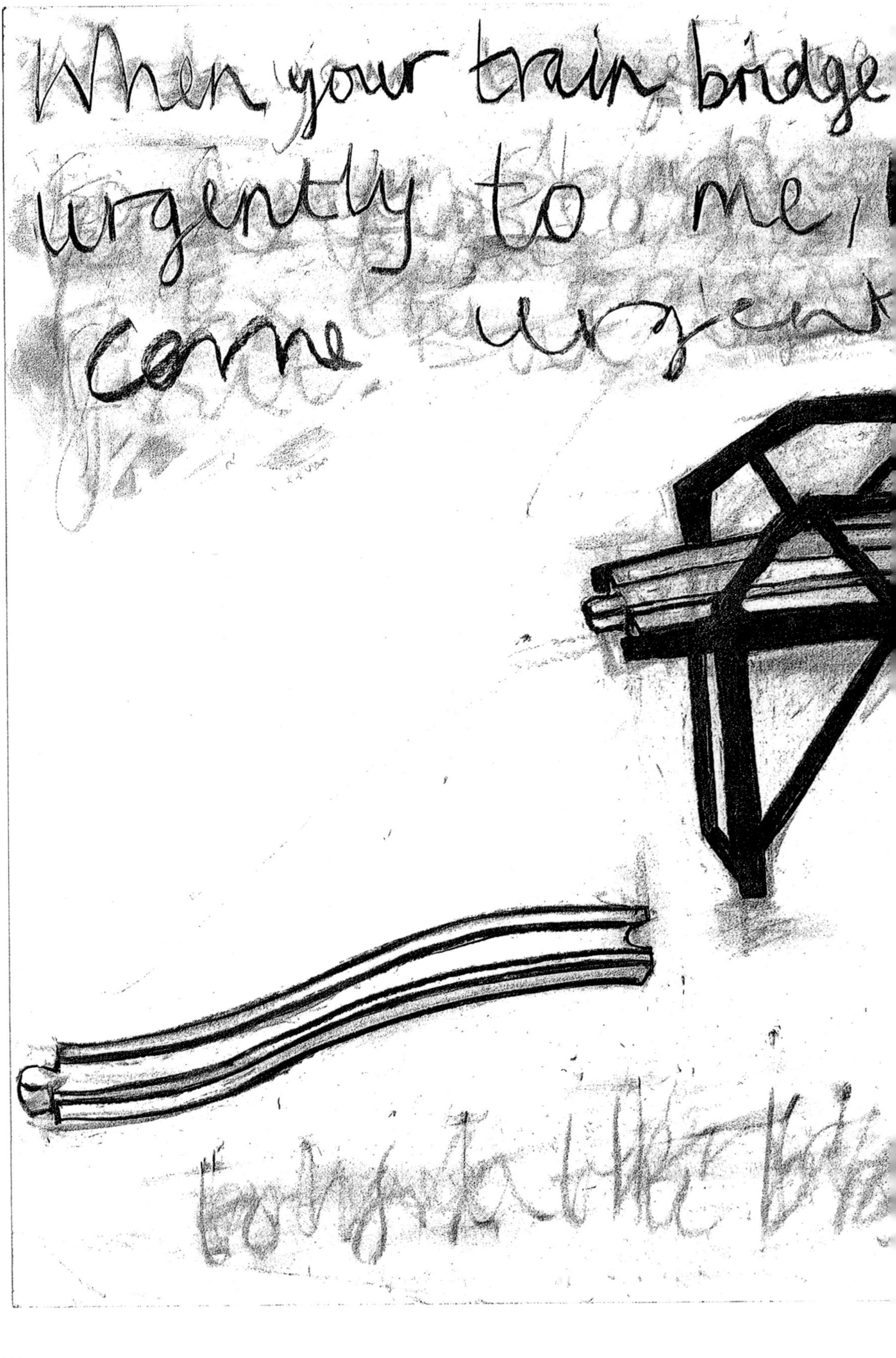
When your train bridge
urgently to me,
Come urgen

breaks you call
simply nust-
uy, right now

And I six

There, young Sarah, hang on, see what you'll become.

it,

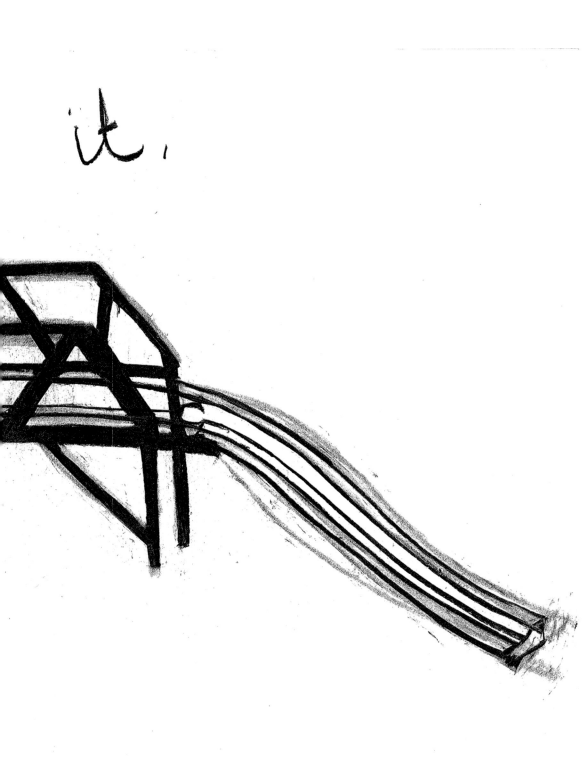

I was waiting for you all along.

APOCRYPHA

THANK YOU

to Harry and Charlie for their love and support, and
to Monika and Shannon for their help with Harry

to Corinne for her belief in the project, and excellent editing

to Woodrow for his skilful and transformative design work

to Candida and the Myriad and New Internationalist team,
and Kendra and the staff of Penn State University Press

to the Laydeez do Comics family,
Ariel, Ariela, Bernard, Bonnie, Deborah, Federica, Maureen, Nancy,
Nicola, Sarah D., Sarah O, Sue C-J, the world of Graphic Medicine

to the teachers and tutors who chose to care,
and to the friends who were also my teachers

to Laura Levitt, whose book 'Jews and Feminism' about 'the
interplay between the need to hold on to and the need to let go
of the places, relationships, and traditions we call home'
held so many resonances for me.

SARAH LIGHTMAN is a London-based artist,
curator, editor and writer. Her artwork has been exhibited in museums
and galleries internationally. She is co-founder of the influential forum
Laydeez do Comics and an Honorary Research Fellow in the School of Arts
at Birkbeck College, University of London. *Graphic Details: Jewish Women's
Confessional Comics* (McFarland 2014) was awarded The Susan Koppelman
Prize for Best Feminist Anthology (2015), The Will Eisner Award for Best
Scholarly Publication (2015) and received an Association of Jewish Studies
Jordan Schnitzer Book Award (2016).

ALLEN ST 160

coffee eggs
and
toast

RIVINGTON ST

and grape jelly
8 years since I
left us the last
time...
who'd belie[ve]
there would b[e]
a day I would com[e]
to the city and neve[r]
tell you I was ther[e]